SINGAPORE
PERSPECTIVES 2018
Together

SINGAPORE
PERSPECTIVES 2018
Together

Edited by

Christopher Gee
Yvonne Arivalagan
Chao Fengqing

Institute of Policy Studies, Singapore

Lee Kuan Yew
School of Public Policy
National University of Singapore

iPS Institute of
Policy Studies

World Scientific

Published by

World Scientific Publishing Co. Pte. Ltd.

5 Toh Tuck Link, Singapore 596224

USA office: 27 Warren Street, Suite 401-402, Hackensack, NJ 07601

UK office: 57 Shelton Street, Covent Garden, London WC2H 9HE

British Library Cataloguing-in-Publication Data

A catalogue record for this book is available from the British Library.

SINGAPORE PERSPECTIVES 2018
Together

ISBN 978-981-3276-25-3 (pbk)

For any available supplementary material, please visit
https://www.worldscientific.com/worldscibooks/10.1142/11155#t=suppl

Desk Editor: Sandhya Venkatesh

Contents

Preface

JANADAS DEVAN

We return this year to a one-word theme for Singapore Perspectives —
"Together". Last year's was two words — "What If?" — unlike the previous
five: "Inequality" in 2012, "Governance" in 2013, "Differences", "Choices"
and "We" in the following years.

Looking back on this series over seven years, it occurs to me they disclose
a certain obsession. Again and again, IPS has returned to the potential fault
lines in our society. We were among the first institutions here to look at the
question of income inequality — that was in 2012. We have returned
repeatedly to questions of racial and religious diversities; of gender and
sexuality too; and of class and social mobility. In other words, how our
diversities can be a bane; of how they might be a strength; of what might
divide us; and of how we might be kept together.

These obsessions are in keeping with IPS's research agenda, which
consists of

1) Managing diversities of all kinds — both what we are familiar with
(race, religion, language) as well as newly emergent ones (like sexuality);

2) Managing the challenges of an ageing society; and also how we might
exploit and accentuate the benefits of an ageing society;

3) Inequality and social mobility; and

4) Governance of a global city-state — the problems peculiar to a city-
state, of which Singapore is the pre-eminent and almost sole example
in the world today.

What I would like to do in this opening is frame the demographic issues
we will discuss today in the context of Singapore being a city-state. For it is
crucial we recognise the centrality of this island-nation being a city when we

consider questions pertaining to our population. We are not an ageing society in a large country. We are not a society trying to accommodate a large immigrant population in a country with lots of space. We are not an advanced global city with a large hinterland. We are but a city-state; we are *only* a city-state.

I touched on this subject in last year's Singapore Perspectives, and will repeat some of the points I made then.

Singapore is a country as well as a city. We don't always keep this obvious fact foremost in our minds — we forget — but Singapore is a city that happens also to be a country; a country that is only a city; a country that has no country — as in "country-side" — outside the city. Or to put it differently, there is no country beyond this city; this city is all the country that we have. This fact informs — consciously and unconsciously; perceptibly and imperceptibly — every facet of our existence. This is how I illustrated this point last year.

One, Singapore is the only city in the world that has a military. London doesn't have a Navy; we do. Tokyo doesn't have an Air Force; we do. Shanghai doesn't have an Army or Terrexes, for that matter; we do.

Two, all of Singapore's gateways — its port, its airport — have to be located within the city. You can't put Changi Airport, for instance, somewhere out in the boondocks, a couple or so hours outside the city — like Narita or Heathrow or KLIA — for the simple reason Singapore doesn't have a boondock. You disembark at our gateways and you're already within the city; not so much as a drawbridge or a moat separates the city walls from the outside.

Three, unusual among global cities, Singapore has a sizeable manufacturing base — 20 per cent of our GDP. There are a number of reasons why this should be so but one is because we are a city as well as a country. If we were to have a purely service economy — like London or New York or other global cities, with high-paying jobs in finance and banking at one end and low-paying jobs flipping hamburgers and providing in-situ services at the other — our income inequalities would be far worse. Indeed, our Gini coefficient is already high — but compared to other countries. When compared to other global cities, we are considerably better off — in large part because we have a substantial manufacturing base providing a range of jobs in the middle.

Now, guess how much land — physical space — do these three activities, which this city has to undertake because it is also a country, occupy: Military (for training, airbases, naval bases); Gateways (airport, port); Manufacturing?

Whenever I ask this question of students or civil servants, the guesses vary from 15% to 25%. The correct answer is 42-43%. That's right, just a little less than half of this not considerable little red dot — and I've not included the land that we have to devote to water reservoirs (5%), housing (17%), roads and rail (13%), parks and nature reserves (9%), and all the other accoutrements of civilised existence — almost half of this city's land area has to be devoted to functions that we have to perform because this city is also a country.

You see, Singapore is a most unlikely country. There is no other city of this size in the world that is also a country. That is why our founding fathers, every one of them, began their political lives believing Singapore, a city, couldn't survive on its own, that it had to be joined to a hinterland, Malaya; and believing that, they fought for Merger, only to be ejected from Malaysia after less than two years, to become a country with no country-side, a city-state with no hinterland. That Singapore should exist — as a city and a country — is a miracle.

But it is a miracle that contains a contradiction inherent in it being both a city and a country. And sustaining this miracle means somehow straddling this contradiction, riding it, managing it — not overcoming it, as such, for it cannot be overcome so long as we remain a sovereign city-state. Let me illustrate the contradiction:

Japan as we know is a rapidly ageing society. Indeed, its population shrank by 400,000 last year. If current trends continue, its population will shrink further, from 126.5 million now, to 88 million by 2065 and only 50 million a hundred years from now.

Note, I said Japan, not Tokyo — which isn't shrinking, as yet. Japan is facing an existential crisis. But I dare say there will still be a Japan if there were only 50 million Japanese, as indeed was the case at the beginning of the last century. But there can be no city — a global city, Tokyo — that shrinks at this rate. Ditto Singapore.

Another illustration: take the question of "talent", which has become something of a dirty word in Singapore by dint of it having been associated with "foreign" for some time.

Why should cities exist? Why did they come into existence in the course of human history over the last 5,000 years or so, and continued to thrive despite the countless calamities that have visited them — from volcanic eruptions and great fires to epidemics; from aerial bombings to tsunamis and earthquakes? What is their evolutionary advantage?

Cities exist primarily because they are a social formation that bring together large numbers of people. That collection of large numbers in close proximity enables the efficient mobilisation and organisation of resources, including of capital and above all of talent. That was as true of Mohenjo-Daro in 2500 BCE or the Rome of Augustus Caesar around the time of Christ as it is today of London and New York. The most thriving global cities tend also to be the most diverse, the most open and dynamic, the most cosmopolitan. Cities often consist of large numbers of "rootless" people, as they say; or at the very least, large segments of their population are "mobile" or "itinerant".

This is of course more true of modern cities; and among contemporary cities, more true of larger metropolitan centres than of smaller cities. But it was true in some respects of even cities in the past. For example, William Shakespeare was born in Stratford-upon-Avon; moved to London to earn a living as an actor and playwright; only to move back to the relatively bucolic setting of Stratford in his retirement. I dare say, if Singapore had remained a part of Malaysia, many of us here may well have retired to Kuantan or Mersing or Langkawi. But we are now only a city, and we can't locate so much as a nursing home for old folks outside this country.

Now, the words I have used to describe the city and city-life — rootless, mobile, itinerant people; diverse, cosmopolitan, dynamic; open to the world and welcoming of all talent — all these terms do not necessarily describe a country. Indeed, countries tend to be altogether more stable entities. They change, certainly; but not as rapidly as cities. They can be diverse; but not as vibrantly and confusingly so as cities. They can have multiple identities; but they are not as bewilderingly diffuse as cities. Think the United States; and think New York City, which only legally and politically belongs to the US. Culturally and spiritually, it lives on another plane. Ditto United Kingdom and London; China and Shanghai; Japan and Tokyo. Countries tend to be oriented inwards, towards themselves; cities tend to be oriented outwards, towards others.

Preface

What happens in the case of city-states — in the case of Singapore? Our identity is forever bifurcated between the global and the local. There is a part of Singapore that is outward looking, cosmopolitan, open; and there is another that is more oriented towards itself, if not insular; more inward focussed, if not closed. We have geographic short-hands for these two Singapores: the Singapore of Shenton Way and the financial district; and the Singapore of the heartlands. The Singapore of Clarke Quay (where I work) feels very different from the Singapore of Toa Payoh (where I live). I rub shoulders with New York, London, Shanghai and Tokyo at Clarke Quay; I feel at home in Toa Payoh.

I can describe the political, economic and social contradiction between these two Singapores briefly thus: If this island-nation does not remain one of the world's leading global cities, it cannot survive as an economy; we might as well not have left Malaysia. To sustain itself as a leading global city, Singapore must remain open to the world, welcome all varieties of talents, become and remain a cosmopolitan society and culture.

To remain a nation, however, Singapore cannot be forever turned determinedly outwards. It cannot be so porous to the outside as to allow itself to be overwhelmed by the foreign. And it cannot resign itself to a diffuse and rootless cosmopolitanism. Life exists here and now, in a particular place and time, or it cannot exist at all. The global economy doubtless exists, but there is no *socius*, no society, no community that answers to it. Singapore, this island-nation, is here, now, and forever.

How do you reconcile this Singapore of home and nation with that other equally real, equally crucial, equally urgent and insistent global and cosmopolitan Singapore? You earn a living, survive, in the latter; you have your home, your being, in the former.

What happened with Brexit in the United Kingdom can happen here. What happened with the election of Donald Trump as US President can also happen here. In Brexit, the city (London) voted overwhelmingly for Europe and globalisation, while the rest of the country thought Britain could go it alone. In the tragic US 2016 Presidential elections, while both the east and west coasts, as well as almost all major urban centres, voted overwhelmingly for the Democratic Hillary Clinton, the rest of the country (fly-over country, the coastal elites used to sniff) voted for the Republican Donald Trump. On one side, the parts of America that benefitted from globalisation and trade — the high tech, connected, cosmopolitan America; and the other, the parts of America that didn't benefit from globalisation and trade, the people who had lost their jobs to foreign competition, the people whom Hillary Clinton had referred to as the "basket of deplorables" — good, ordinary, decent people who happened to feel, with good reason, that they were being looked down upon, ignored by the globalised coastal elites — they voted for the boorish Donald Trump.

The same divisions can happen here — within the same city, between the two Singapores. And the divisions between the two Singapores can be accentuated by differences of class — and of race too, if the class divisions coincide with racial ones. It can also be accentuated by differences of age, with the young seeing their future in an open and globalised Singapore and their elders seeing theirs in a Singapore that is relatively more closed and more stable; with the young choosing, as in Brexit, a future-directed, forward-thrusting productive economy and their elders preferring instead consumption.

This is why this conference on our demographic challenges is entitled "Together". For it seems to me self-evident that unless we take great pains to remain together our society too can fracture. This is why I believe Government should be the place where people are brought together. Why I believe our politics and policy must always keep their eyes trained on keeping us together. For the alternative is unthinkable. The city, Singapore, cannot separate from the country, Singapore.

Acknowledgements

IPS is grateful to the following institutions
for their support of Singapore Perspectives 2018.

ENGRO
BUILDING SUSTAINABILITY

Keppel Corporation

Singtel

TEMASEK

ascendas
SINGBRIDGE

CHANGI
airport group

DBS

FN FRASER AND NEAVE, LIMITED

HOUSING &
DEVELOPMENT
BOARD

INFOCOMM
MEDIA
DEVELOPMENT
AUTHORITY

ITE
Institute of Technical Education

KHONG GUAN 康元

M P A
SINGAPORE

MAS
Monetary Authority
of Singapore

NYP NANYANG
THE INNOVATIVE POLYTECHNIC

NANYANG
TECHNOLOGICAL
UNIVERSITY
SINGAPORE

SUSS
SINGAPORE UNIVERSITY
OF SOCIAL SCIENCES

SUTD
SINGAPORE UNIVERSITY OF
TECHNOLOGY AND DESIGN

Temasek
POLYTECHNIC

THAKRAL
CORPORATION LTD

UOB

Introduction

CHRISTOPHER GEE

I would like you to think about this tension that I feel (and I believe this is shared by many of us) between the principle of self-reliance and individual responsibility on the one hand, with the notion of the collective, a social state where people depend on one another.

These two concepts, seemingly contradictory, run through all the scenarios and policies we will discuss today. They lie at the heart of our responses and choice-making as we confront our demographic destiny.

Narratives of Singapore's demographic destiny are often almost apocalyptic, described with terms like Demographic Time-Bomb, Demographic Bust, and a Silver Tsunami. Demographers and social scientists also bandy about terms like old-age dependency or burden that frame the outlook from a negative, glass half-empty perspective.

But alternative narratives exist. The elderly population are also solutions, productive resources that remain available to our society. Strong social safety nets already exist and may be extended further.

Whilst we have already benefitted from a first demographic dividend, there are other dividends that may be harnessed. Having a realistic and balanced perspective of our demographic challenges is a necessary first step in the journey towards solutions.

Singapore has to manage these challenges of an ageing population in its context as a city-state with an open economy, only 720 square kilometres, with no hinterland full of young citizens wanting to seize opportunities in the city, and for older people to retire to have a more affordable, less frenetic lifestyle.

Everything in this city-state is more concentrated, with density increasing competition for resources. Cities are very unequal places. Diversity combines with density to intensify contestation, between incumbents and newcomers, potentially also between young and old. Are we to add generational divides to our already long list of differences in our people?

Singapore's first demographic dividend was captured in the late sixties onwards. The share of the working age population rose quickly and by 2000 had contributed almost 3% points per annum to GDP per capita growth over three decades, more than one-third of per capita growth in that period.

However, the declining fertility that gave rise to the first dividend also causes its reversal — the effects of the first dividend began to reverse in the mid-2000s, and now acts as a drag on GDP per capita growth of minus 1.5% points per annum into the future.

This is the effective cost of our ageing population, assuming things like labour force participation rates and wages remain the same. This, then, is the demographic bust scenario.

But societies can adapt. Rational individuals, anticipating longer lives, have greater incentives to invest in human and economic capital to increase productive potential. There are other pay-offs from living longer: health, education and savings.

Improved healthspan, which is the number of years lived in a healthy state, could add to the number of productive life years of older Singaporeans. For example, the number of Singaporeans aged 65 and above will be close to a million by 2030, but if the health trends in the last ten years can be sustained, there will be an extra 450,000 healthy person years in that cohort, representing a pool of productive human capital equivalent to 20% of our resident workforce today. Many of these older Singaporeans will be much more highly educated than the generation immediately before.

We can also deploy our accumulated household savings, totalling 2 trillion dollars-worth into productive investments to generate income to help us pay for our consumption in old-age. These amounts complement public sector savings, or our national reserves, which can and are invested to generate income to help pay for our fiscal spending needs (this is the Net Investment Returns Contribution to the government's annual budget).

Investments into technology and innovation can boost these longevity dividends further, but could also yield unequal outcomes. The immediate impact of new disruptive technologies is likely to affect older workers most.

So how can our society best adapt to population ageing? Immigration can offset some of the quantity effects of population ageing, and with appropriate calibration can help to fill resource gaps in the domestic workforce. Analysis we've conducted shows that in-migration has deferred the point at which population ageing takes effect on economic growth.

However, immigrants also get old. An ever-larger intake of immigrants will be required to maintain economic growth. Immigration cannot be the only answer therefore.

The longevity dividends highlighted earlier, combined with technology, can boost individuals' capacity to provide for themselves in old-age, but these can be regressive without appropriate socio-economic policy interventions.

In Singapore, family is recognised as the main source of social support, but in the future more and more elderly Singaporeans will have little or no family support.

Other transfer mechanisms to help us finance old-age consumption include tax-financed public transfers, where taxes on mainly working age persons are levied to help pay for subsidies and rebates on goods and services for the elderly. Higher taxes will have an effect on economic competitiveness, which is important in a city-state like ours with an open economy.

Social risk-pooling is another transfer mechanism. These are schemes, such as CPF LIFE or MediShield Life, that help individuals hedge longevity risks. These social risk-pooling schemes could be extended into other domains, such as long-term care or employment, or even to hedge the risk of outliving our leasehold housing assets.

All these mechanisms that can help offset the effects of population ageing are dependent on the level of intergenerational solidarity in our society. Our choices about our preferred transfer mechanisms (family, social risk-pooling or taxation) and the effectiveness of savings-driven investments will depend on how much we care for a shared future together, both within our current generation as well as future generations.

To this end the IPS conducted a survey on Attitudes towards Intergenerational Solidarity, amongst other matters. This survey of 2000 Singaporean citizens and PRs was completed last month, and asked respondents for their views on this topic of generational support.

We posed a question on whether each generation should take care of itself, rather than be supported by other generations, testing notions of self-reliance versus intergenerational support. Respondents were split. 41% agreed with the concept of generational self-reliance, but a surprisingly high 38% disagreed, with proportionately more of the young (who might be expected to have to take care of the old) disagreeing that each generation should take care of itself.

In contrast to our Many Helping Hands approach for social support, respondents ranked government as next in line, after family, to take care of the elderly, as opposed to community. Is this a reflection of greater expectation of the government, or the perception of the relative capabilities of the respective sectors today?

The risk of outliving one's retirement savings may be forcing those in their fifties and early sixties to reserve assets for their own old-age financial security, instead of leaving them as an inheritance.

Higher spending on the elderly has been predicted with the ageing population. We asked respondents in our survey how this might be paid for, higher taxes or tapping on national reserves. Whilst we also had a mixed response to these questions, slightly more disagreed to paying higher taxes, with those in the 45-64 year age group more likely to disagree to higher taxes.

This is unsurprising, as they are the ones who pay the most tax, but who also may have the responsibility of caring for both the young and the old.

Although more on balance agreed to using more of the returns from investing national reserves to fund social spending on the elderly today, there was a high proportion of neutral responses to this rather difficult question.

Respondents in our survey, across the different age groups, had the view that older workers (aged 55 and above) experience age discrimination when looking for jobs. Age discrimination would be a major barrier to efforts to increase older workers' employment and raise their productive potential, and prevent us from increasing the dynamism of our economy.

In summary, Singapore has had the benefit of a powerful first demographic dividend, which is now unwinding as the population ages. There are however large pay-offs if we are able to harness other longevity dividends through investments in human and economic capital, especially in healthspan, education and by deploying accumulated savings in productive investments.

Transfer mechanisms such as tax-financed subsidies or social risk-pooling schemes can in the meantime also help us to finance old-age consumption and pool our longevity risks. Ultimately though, it is our values, choices and our collective mind-set that will help us determine our demographic destiny together.

I come back then to the contradiction I posed at the start: of that tension between the self-reliant individual, with the concept of a community, sharing its risks and opportunities. You've heard that these ideas underpin the necessary societal adaptations to ageing, but I wonder whether if this framing is a false dichotomy.

There need NOT be any conflict between these two concepts, and the society that manages to marry the two will manage the challenges of ageing the best: self-reliant, resilient citizens pooling their lifecycle risks, and sharing their futures with future Singaporean generations, all together.

I

The Singapore Economy: Ageing yet Dynamic?

CHAPTER 1

Economic Dynamism Amidst Demographic Change

RAVI MENON

I will focus my presentation on the economic implications of demographic change: what it means for economic growth and economic dynamism. The two are different. My presentation will centre around two broad themes. First, I will describe our demographic trilemma — the constraints and the choices we need to make. Second, I would like to argue that demographics is not destiny — why economic dynamism is not a numbers game and how we can remain dynamic amidst this demographic challenge.

Decline in fertility has dragged down resident population growth

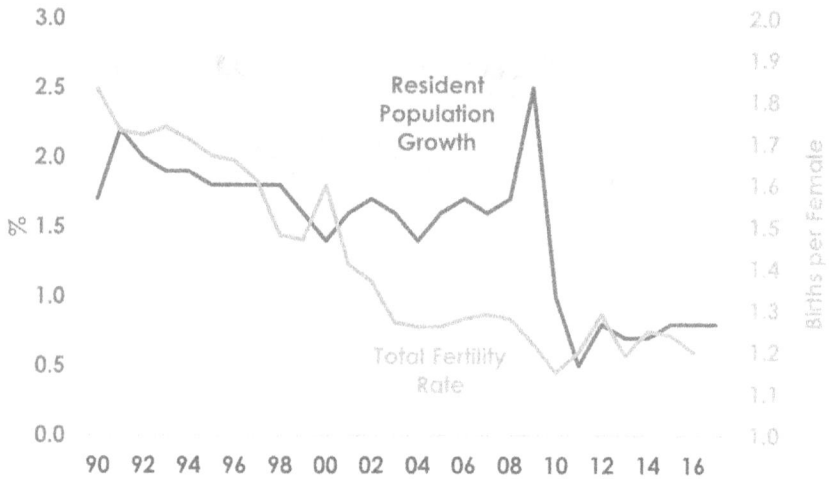

Source: Department of Statistics

Let's start with the total fertility rate, or TFR. By the way, we must be one of the few countries in the world where most people know what TFR stands for! It is indeed an existential issue for us. The TFR is the starting point of all demographic analysis. Singapore has had a sustained decline in its TFR. Our TFR fell from around 1.8 in the 1980s (which is already below the replacement level of 2.1) to about 1.3 in the early 2000s. This has weighed heavily on resident population growth as seen from the relatively close correlation with the TFR. There appears to be three distinct phases in the last 30 years. In the 1990s, both the TFR and resident population growth declined in tandem. In the 2000s, the TFR continued to decline but resident population growth recovered. This reflected net positive immigration as the number of new citizens and permanent residents grew. In this decade, the TFR appears to have stabilised at around 1.2–1.3 while resident population growth fell sharply reflecting the tightening of immigration flows.

Assuming zero net migration, working-age population will start to shrink soon

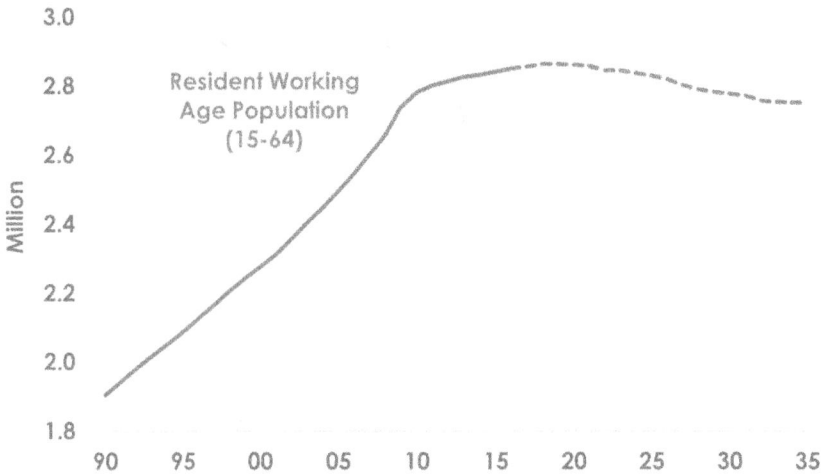

Source: Estimates from Department of Statistics Singapore and Monetary Authority of Singapore

The next two slides are a thought experiment. They are not a forecast or prediction but aim to illustrate the implications of having very low resident population growth. First, let us assume that we have zero net immigration starting from this year. The resident working-age population — this is defined as citizens and permanent residents between the ages of 15 to 64 — will begin to shrink from around 2020. The exact year is not key. What is important to note is that it is not far off. By 2035, the working-age resident population will possibly decline by a cumulative 3.5 per cent.

Assuming zero increase in foreign workers, labour force will similarly decline

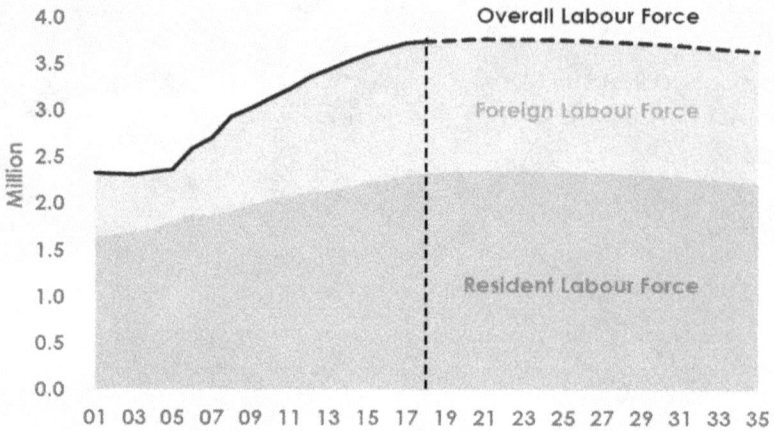

Source: Estimates from Ministry of Manpower and Monetary Authority of Singapore

Second, let us assume zero net increase in foreign workers from now on. The overall labour force will decline gradually from around 2022, driven fundamentally by the shrinking resident labour force.

If labour force declines*, GDP growth will also decline

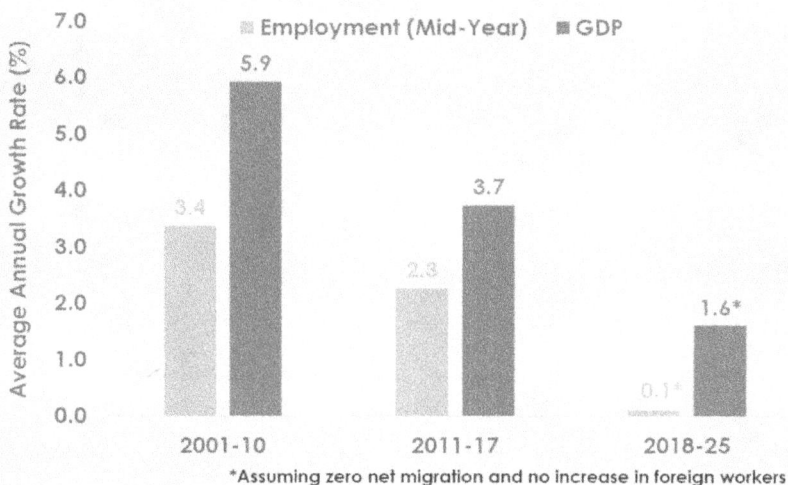

Employment (Mid-Year) ■ GDP

*Assuming zero net migration and no increase in foreign workers

Source: Estimates from the Department of Statistics, Ministry of Manpower and Monetary Authority of Singapore

These two assumptions taken together — zero net migration (i.e., no additional new citizens or permanent residents on a net basis) and no additional foreign workers — will have important implications for economic growth. From the perspective of the supply-side capacity or potential of the economy, GDP growth can be seen as the sum of productivity growth and labour force growth. This means, holding productivity growth constant, a decline in labour force growth will have a direct impact on economic growth. This correlation appears to be borne out in the past empirically. If labour force growth falls to near zero, then the only source of GDP growth is productivity growth. If productivity growth stays at about 1.5 per cent, which is what we have likely averaged over the last seven years (based on mid-year employment), then GDP growth will approach that level.

The demographic trilemma

Zero
Net Immigration

Stable Foreign
Worker Share

Positive Labour Force Growth

This then is the demographic trilemma. We have three possible objectives that various people in Singapore have advocated in the past. The reality is, at any one time, we can achieve only two out of the three objectives.

The three possible objectives are:

- Positive labour force expansion
- Zero net immigration, that some would prefer
- No increase in share of foreign workers in total workforce

So, what are the trade-offs? If you look at the corners of the triangle, that's where the trade-offs are: If we want labour force to grow and have zero net immigration, then we have to allow the share of foreign workers in the workforce to rise. That's the bottom left of the triangle. If we want the overall labour force to grow and the share of foreign workers to be stable, then we have to allow net immigration. That's the bottom right of the triangle. If we want zero net immigration and the foreign worker share to be stable, then we have to accept zero labour force growth. That's the top of the triangle.

The trilemma represents the constraints. I've put them in rather stark terms, to reflect vividly the trade-offs we face. Collectively, as a society, we have to decide which corner of the trilemma we want to be at, or which corner we want to be close to. I'll argue later on that we may be able to soften these constraints and reach more balanced outcomes. But the fundamental constraints and choices implied by the trilemma are real.

A recovery in fertility is the best solution but will help only in the long run

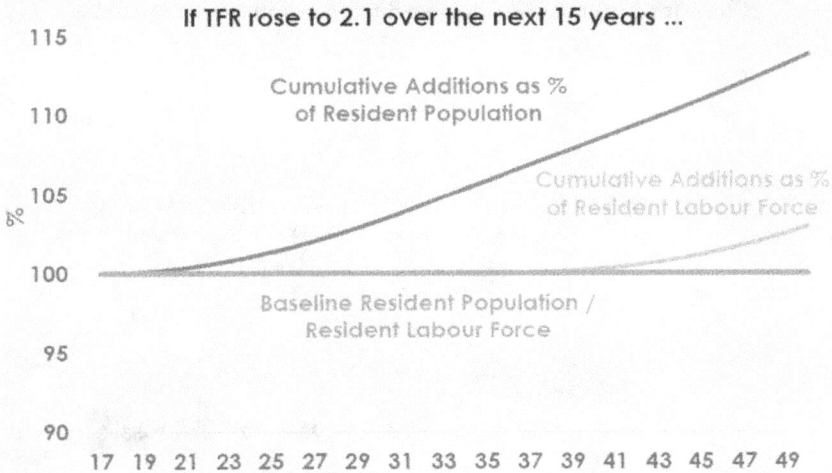

If TFR rose to 2.1 over the next 15 years ...

Cumulative Additions as %
of Resident Population

Cumulative Additions as %
of Resident Labour Force

Baseline Resident Population /
Resident Labour Force

Source: Estimates from the Monetary Authority of Singapore

Are there ways to escape the trilemma? Or at least soften its hard constraints? There are two solutions that have often been mentioned. First, an increase in fertility. Second, an increase in resident labour force participation rate. A recovery in Singapore's TFR is the best and most lasting solution that we can have, but its positive effects on labour force will only occur in the very long run.

So here's another thought experiment: Assume our TFR rises steadily from the current level of 1.2 to 2.1 (replacement rate) over next 15 years. Obviously, it will have an immediate impact on resident population and its effect will cumulate over time. That is shown by the blue line which is shooting up quite nicely. But crucially a recovery in the TFR will not have any perceptible impact on labour force and GDP growth until nearly 2040. This is shown by the yellow line. It will take time for the extra babies born in the next 15 years to start entering the labour force. So while it's the most lasting solution to our challenges, TFR effects will only impact the economy in the long run.

Improvements in labour force participation will help in the near term but not by much

If gender gap in LFPR narrowed to German levels by 2035 ...

Source: Estimates from the Monetary Authority of Singapore

The second way to soften the trilemma is to increase our resident Labour Force Participation Rate (LFPR). This will have more immediate payoffs. But even at plausible stretch targets, its effects on resident labour force growth will be quite limited. Singapore's LFPR — defined as share of the resident population aged 15–64 who are in the labour force — is currently 76.1. It is not bad by OECD standards but there is scope to improve it. Japan is at 76.8; Germany is at 77.9; the Netherlands is at 79.9; Sweden is at 82.1.

Our LFPR for older workers is not bad; it is female LFPR where we are lagging behind. There is currently still a fairly large gender LFPR gap between male and females in their 40s and 50s. This gap in Singapore is higher than that in leading OECD countries. In many advanced economies, women tend to return to the work force after their prime child-bearing years. In Singapore, this is much less prevalent. If we can make it easier for our women to return to the workforce after they have had their children, we can narrow the gender gap vis-à-vis the advanced economies.

This slide demonstrates another thought experiment. Assume we narrow our gender gap from the current 15 percentage points to 11 percentage points by 2035 — approximately the level seen in Germany and Netherlands. This will only translate into a cumulative labour force increase of about 2 per cent in 2035.

How can we soften the hard constraints of the demographic trilemma?

1   **Make it easier to set up a family; make it easier for women to return to workforce**

2   **Seek balanced solutions – some net immigration, some increase in labour force, some flexibility in foreign worker share**

3   **Focus on size and type of foreign workforce that will maximise job and wage opportunities for Singaporeans**

The demographic trilemma presents the constraints and choices facing us. We can soften it by raising the TFR and LFPR. Of course, having babies or returning to work are deeply personal choices. No one makes these choices in order to boost labour force growth or GDP growth, and we should not suggest doing so. The government tries to facilitate fertility and labour force participation because that is what many people desire for their own fulfilment. Many women would like to return to work, but they face a number of constraints. We must make it easier for them to do so. The government has made significant efforts in recent years to invest in childcare and facilitate more flexible working arrangements. We must continue to push on this front and collectively as a society enable more who want to work enter the workforce.

Likewise, many married couples want to have children — not for GDP but because children are a source of joy and fulfilment of love. Government policies on marriage and parenthood are guided by this higher purpose. And of course, a growing labour force is a happy, economic by-product.

We must make balanced choices in addressing the trilemma. We must accept a slower rate of labour force growth. The underlying demographic slowdown is so severe that it is neither feasible nor desirable to try to completely offset it through immigration or foreign workers. But we must also allow a certain rate of net immigration to augment our resident population. This is not just about numbers but about rejuvenation and expanding our talent base. And while we cannot keep increasing our share of foreign workforce indefinitely, we must be flexible in allowing fluctuations in the ratio according to economic cycles, changing circumstances, and opportunities.

Finally, we must reframe our question on foreign workers. It is not about how many foreign workers industry wants or society can afford to have, but what number and kind of foreign workers we need to maximise the job and wage opportunities for Singaporeans. Foreign workers must be a complement to the local workforce.

Let me move on to the second broad theme — that demographics is not destiny. We can sustain our economic dynamism in the face of demographic change.

We cannot grow as fast as before ...

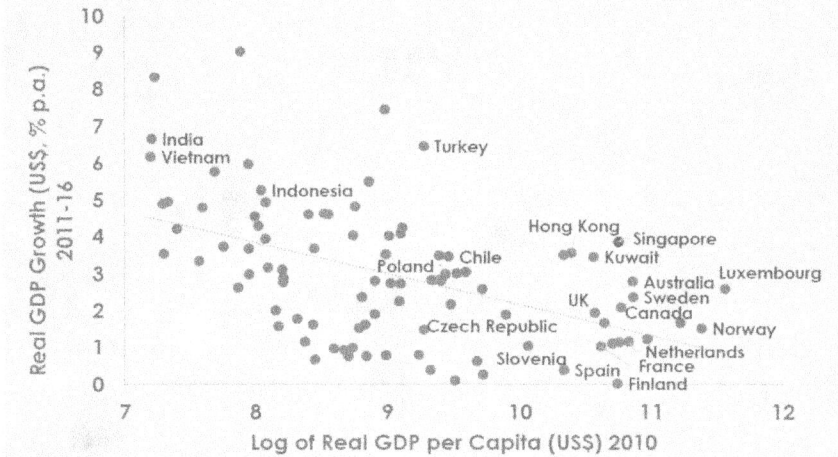

Source: World Bank, World Development Indicators

First, we should not grow despondent over our slowing rate of economic growth. The empirical experience of countries over time shows a negative relationship between level of income and the growth of income. It is not a perfect negative relationship as you can see from the scatter but it suggests that countries with low levels of GDP per capita tend to have higher rates of GDP growth. This is called "catch-up" in the literature.

Meanwhile, countries with higher levels of GDP per capita tend to grow at slower rates as they are more mature. Singapore is a mature economy as you can see; it has one of the highest levels of per capita income in the world. We will not be able to sustain the 6–7 per cent rates of growth that were seen a decade ago. And there's nothing to be unhappy about this. In fact, our position above the downward sloping line in the slide shows that we have managed to grow faster in recent years than countries with similar levels of per capita income.

... but as a city we cannot afford to grow too slowly either

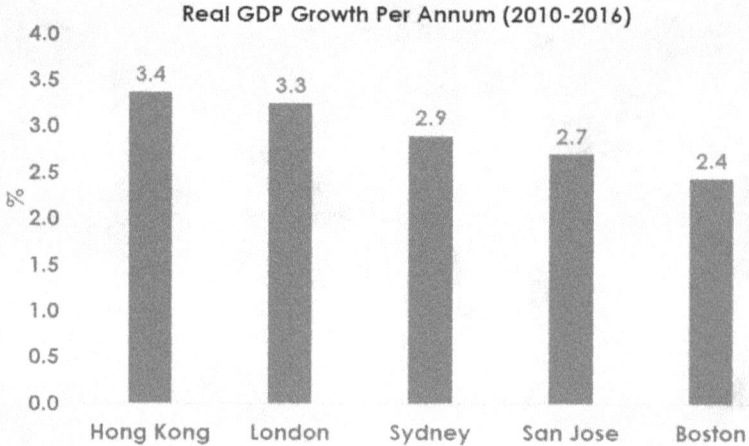

Real GDP Growth Per Annum (2010-2016)

City	Growth (%)
Hong Kong	3.4
London	3.3
Sydney	2.9
San Jose	2.7
Boston	2.4

Source: U.S. Bureau of Economic Analysis, Office for National Statistics (U.K.), Haver Analytics, SGS Economic & Planning, Monetary Authority of Singapore

But while we must accept a lower rate of growth than before, as a global city, we cannot afford to grow too slowly either. It seems many leading global cities grow at rates between 2.5–3.5 per cent, faster than the national average of the countries they are a part of. London has averaged 3.3 per cent annual growth since the financial crisis while Sydney has averaged around 2.9 per cent. San Jose (which encompasses Silicon Valley) has averaged 2.7 per cent per annum.

It is hard to imagine a dynamic city growing at less than 2 per cent or worse still, 1.5 per cent. It will be unattractive to investors and talent, including the city's own investors and talented people. A reasonably good rate of growth helps to create opportunities and preserve a sense of progress and hope, particularly among the young. It will also facilitate upward social mobility.

In leading cities, productivity is the key source of economic growth and dynamism

Sources of GDP Growth (2010-16)

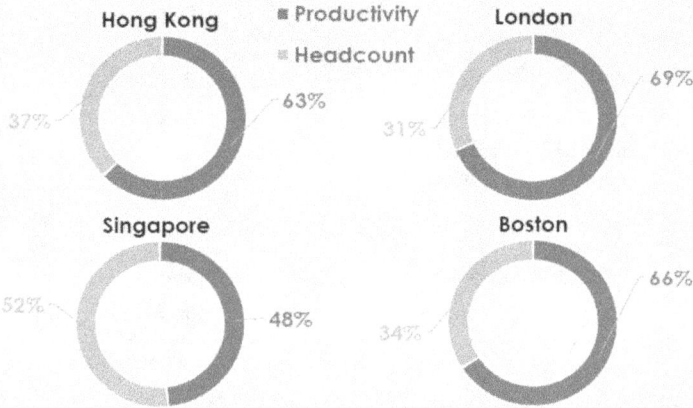

Hong Kong   ■ Productivity   London

■ Headcount

37% 63% 31% 69%

Singapore   Boston

52% 48% 34% 66%

Source: U.S. Bureau of Economic Analysis, Office for National Statistics (U.K.), CEIC, Monetary Authority of Singapore

The experience of other leading cities suggests that demographics is not destiny. Yes, vibrant cities do attract people — and their additions to the labour force add to growth. But the main source of their growth and dynamism is not headcount but productivity.

This is not an in-depth study but it appears that about two-thirds of overall GDP growth in the cities shown is due to productivity improvements. In comparison, productivity has accounted for about half of Singapore's GDP growth. There is clearly scope for us to do better and thereby sustain our dynamism.

Scope to reap human capital dividends

Highest Qualification Attained by Residents 25 Years & Over

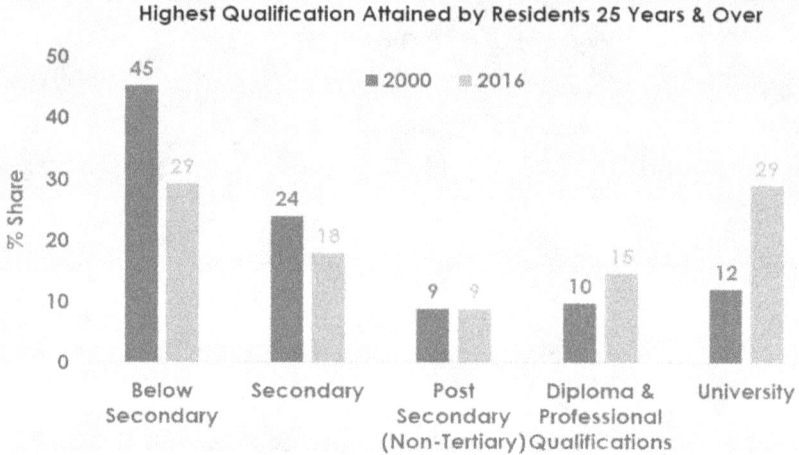

Source: Department of Statistics Singapore

How can we do this?

First, Singapore has scope to reap the human capital dividends that are arising from the continuous investments we have made in education and training in past decades. As recently as 2000, 45 per cent of the resident workforce had below secondary school education, and only 12 per cent had university education. In just one-and-a-half decades, those ratios have converged, reflecting the cumulation of efforts made over preceding decades. The proportion with less than secondary education has dipped below 30 per cent; while the proportion of the university-educated has more than doubled to nearly 30 per cent.

The effects of this transformation in human capital will continue to be felt in the productive capacity of the workforce. With higher levels of education, the ability of the workforce to take on more complex tasks and to leverage on technology is substantially stronger. There is more to come. The share of the university-educated may not continue to as rise sharply but there is still plenty of scope to increase the share of those with secondary, post-secondary and diploma & professional qualifications. They will be better placed to transform the nature of many jobs, raising standards and quality, thus enabling productivity and wages in these occupations to rise.

Scope to improve quality of foreign workforce

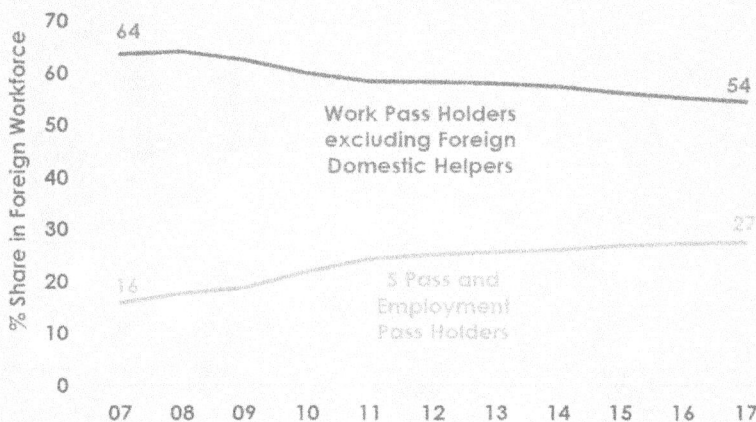

Source: Ministry of Manpower

Second, there is scope to improve the quality of the foreign workforce. We should increasingly be concerned about the skills of the foreign workers that we take in, rather than just the numbers. In fact, more skilled foreign workers will mean that we will need less of them. The trend of improving quality in our foreign workforce has already begun. The proportion of work permit holders has declined by about 10 percentage points over last 10 years, while the proportion of S Pass and employment pass holders has increased by around 10 percentage points. This trend must continue as we restructure our economy towards higher value-added activities, seek deeper skills, and undertake more pervasive digitalisation.

Scope to raise productivity in domestic services jobs

Wage as % of Country's Median Wage

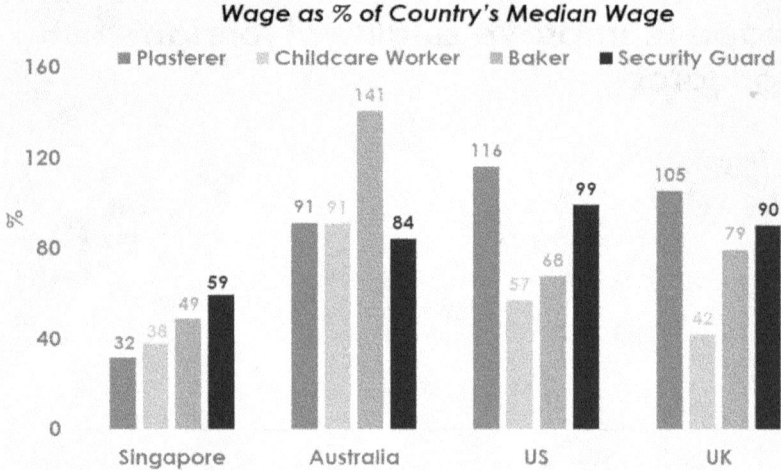

Source: Australian Bureau of Statistics, U.S. Bureau of Labour Statistics, U.K. Office for National Statistics, Ministry of Manpower, Monetary Authority of Singapore

Third, there is scope to increase productivity and efficiency in many domestic services jobs. Consider wages in four occupations (Plasterer, Childcare Worker, Baker, and Security Guard) across four countries (Singapore, Australia, the US, and the UK). The slide shows the median wage in these occupations relative to the overall median wage in that country. In Singapore, the typical pay in these occupations range from 30–60 per cent of the local median wage. In Australia, these occupations have wages much closer to the median wage. Wages in these occupations are also higher in the US and the UK, though the pattern is slightly different across countries. There is scope to further professionalise these jobs in Singapore. In particular, to increase the skills content, leverage on technology, improve business processes, and raise the quality of output. This will enhance productivity and help to support higher wages in these occupations.

Professionalising rank-and-file jobs will broaden and strengthen middle class

Wage as % of Country's Median Wage

■ Bank Teller ■ Vehicle Mechanic ■ Hairdresser ■ Bus Driver

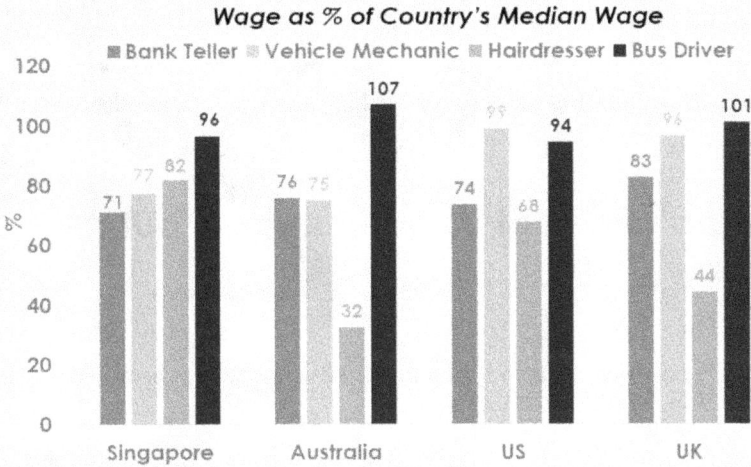

Source: Australian Bureau of Statistics, U.S. Bureau of Labour Statistics, U.K. Office for National Statistics, Ministry of Manpower, Monetary Authority of Singapore

In fact, the professionalisation of more of such so-called "rank-and-file" jobs in Singapore will help to strengthen and broaden the middle class, and make for a more equitable society. And Singapore can do this. We have good examples of jobs that have historically been perceived to be less skilled that have now been successfully upgraded. These jobs now command much relatively good wages, close to that seen in Australia, the US and the UK, controlling for median incomes. This slide shows that our bank tellers, vehicle mechanics, hairdressers, and bus drivers earn a good (median) wage that is quite close to the median. In fact, our bus drivers appear to be paid just below the median in Singapore, comparable to their counterparts in Australia, the US and the UK. And hairdressers in Singapore are doing amazingly well. They earn much closer to the median wage compared to their counterparts in Australia, the US and the UK.

The story of our bus drivers is interesting. Since the introduction of the Bus Contracting Model by the Ministry of Transport and the entrance of foreign bus operators, there has been greater competition in the bus industry, raising the game. Bus driving became more professional. The focus is on driving well, increasing fuel efficiency, and meeting the targets set by the Ministry of Transport on frequency and timeliness. More women have also been drawn into the industry with the introduction of flexible working arrangements and maternity leave. The result is that the dependency on foreign workers has been reduced, and productivity and wages have increased. Now our bus drivers are making close to the median wage in Singapore.

Dynamism is not about numbers but quality

1   Economic dynamism is about efficiency, entrepreneurship, innovation, and talent

2   Internationally competitive advanced manufacturing and modern services complemented by high-quality domestic services

3   An open, resilient, innovative, and inclusive society

In sum, demographics is not destiny and economic dynamism is not about numbers. Dynamism is about quality — the quality of our workforce, the quality of our enterprises, and the quality of our institutions. It is about high levels of efficiency and productivity. It is about growing the Singaporean talent base as well as being a magnet for the world's talents. It is about a vibrant entrepreneurial and innovation base, characterised by a lot of start-ups, a lot of experimentation, and a lot of R&D.

A key aspect of dynamism is also high rates of churn in the labour and capital resources in our firms. There needs to be continuous flux and reallocation of resources in response to changing economic and market conditions. Both capital and labour need to be nimble and highly adaptive. The structure of the Singapore economy is well suited for sustaining our dynamism. Singapore's strong advanced manufacturing and related trade and logistics activities are internationally competitive. In modern services, comprising financial, professional services, and info-communications technology, we enjoy an international hub status. Together, these sectors make up some 40 per cent of our economy. If our domestic services can be further professionalised — job by job, each worker possessing deep skills and delivering a high quality of service, we will be a dynamic economy.

Finally, dynamism must be about our people. We must remain an open society. Not just in being open to foreign trade, investment, and talent, but being deeply connected to the rest of the world. Not just attracting foreign talent to Singapore but Singaporeans venturing abroad as our companies and industries internationalise. Most of all, being open in spirit and mindset, staying open to diversity, being comfortable working in multi-cultural settings, thriving in a globalised world.

We must also remain a resilient society. Able to ride the ups and downs of business cycles and structural changes. Able to adapt, learn new skills, continually improve. We must become a more innovative society to be dynamic. Willing to experiment and accepting failure as a halfway house to success. Investing in R&D, leveraging on technology. Most of all, having an enterprising spirit — always seeking new and better ways to do things.

In the end, we must be an inclusive society. It is probably not a coincidence that IPS has chosen to make the theme of this conference "Together". The two forces that offer the most promise for sustained economic dynamism are globalisation and technology. But how far we can reap the benefits of globalisation and technology will depend on how well we bring all our people together. The path of dynamism is also the path of continuous disruption, even dislocation. To sustain the momentum and consensus in favour of globalisation and technology, we must help those adversely affected by them and equip Singaporeans to succeed. And to maintain cohesion in the face of population ageing and growing healthcare burdens, those who have benefitted from our growth and dynamism must contribute to the larger society — through taxation, philanthropy, community service.

We then become not just a dynamic people but also a compassionate one. Now that is a combination worth having, and I think the only one worth having.

CHAPTER 2

Redesigning Jobs for Our Silver Age to Drive Our Thriving Economy

SEAN TAN

I want to share some practical perspectives on the topic of job redesign, and hopefully, it is useful for organisations who have some interest in the topic of job redesign. I want to focus on three key areas. First of all, why bother about job redesign? Number two, what makes job redesign challenging? Number three, how do we make job redesign really work?

Job redesign is a topic that is drawing increasing interest in recent years and there are several perspectives that are attached to it. Our local population size is about 3.5 million right now, and from 2025, this number is expected to fall gradually. Now, with the dip in overall local population, our local workforce will naturally take a hit. For every one local exiting the workforce due to retirement, there were two locals entering it. This was the reality in 2012.

OUR LABOUR MARKET IS SHRINKING

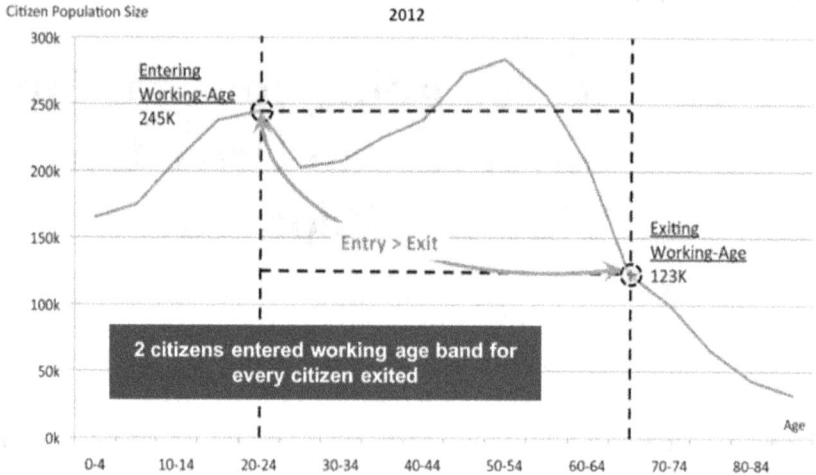

Citizen Population Size

2012

Entering Working-Age 245K

Entry > Exit

Exiting Working-Age 123K

2 citizens entered working age band for every citizen exited

Age

0-4   10-14   20-24   30-34   40-44   50-54   60-64   70-74   80-84

Source: Department of Statistics

If you fast forward to the year 2030 — just about 12 years from now — the picture looks very different. For every one local exiting the workforce, there will only be 0.7 entering it.

OUR LABOUR MARKET IS SHRINKING

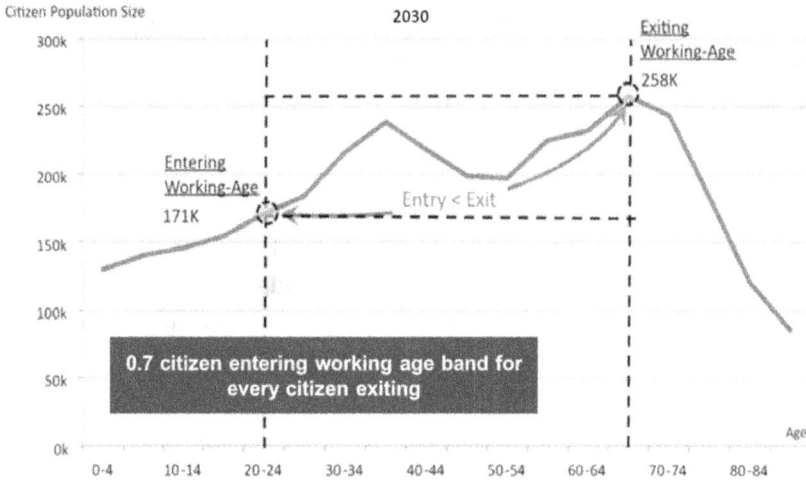

Citizen Population Size

2030

Exiting
Working-Age
258K

Entering
Working-Age
171K

Entry < Exit

300k

250k

200k

150k

100k

50k

0k

0.7 citizen entering working age band for
every citizen exiting

Age

0-4   10-14   20-24   30-34   40-44   50-54   60-64   70-74   80-84

Source: Department of Statistics

With this happening, I think it confirms that our local workforce will indeed shrink. We also know that not only is the workforce shrinking, it is also ageing. In 1970, for every one local who was aged 65 or higher — assuming that this is the proxy retirement age — we had more than 13 people aged between 20 and 64 — deemed as the proxy working age band — supporting that person. This is the old-age support ratio, and it was 13.5 in 1970. Twenty years later, the ratio fell to 10.5. Another 20 years later, the ratio fell to 7.4. Last year in 2017, the ratio fell further to 5.1. Now, come 2030, the ratio will fall to as low as 1:2.1; and this is the year that Changi Airport Terminal 5 will also open for business, and we know about the high level of automation that we can expect.

I think it is going to be interesting and we need to quickly catch up in view of the situation they are looking at right now. Now, if you are around my age — I will probably be on the side of being supported, on the left side of this ratio, come year 2030. I think I will really be appreciative of the opportunity to remain in the workforce for as long as possible so that I can alleviate the financial burden that I will be putting on those who are

31

supporting me. For some of you who are much younger than me, you will probably still be on the supporting side, which is on the right side of this ratio. I think you too will be highly appreciative if those whom you support can remain in the workforce for as long as possible so that your financial load could also be alleviated. Now, irrespective of which side of this ratio we will be on, I believe all of us in this room will have some interest to keep our people in the workforce for as long as possible.

Let us look at some of the economic challenges associated with our labour market situation. Our Manpower Minister, Mr Lim Swee Say, has always been speaking very passionately about these issues. His talking points revolve around our economic growth, productivity and also our foreign worker numbers, particularly how our economic growth in recent years somehow followed workforce growth, suggesting that there is very little productivity uplift in recent times.

GDP growth numbers closely resemble the foreign workforce growth numbers, somehow suggesting that our economic growth is propelled mainly by our growth in the foreign workforce growth numbers, and productivity is flat. Mr Lim also passionately said that continuing to rely on foreign workforce growth to drive our economic growth should not be the solution. Right now, the ratio of foreign to local workforce is about one third foreign, two third local. If the rate of growth in foreign workforce is allowed to continue, we will soon see a reversal of this composition. We will have more foreign workers than local workers in the workforce and this presents a little bit of risk to our economy. Hence, the answer is clear: we need a deliberate plan to drive productivity growth.

OUR DEPENDENCY ON FOREIGN WORKERS

	2012	2013	2014	2015	2016
Resident Workforce	2.12M	2.14M	2.19M	2.23M	2.26M
Foreign Workforce	1.27M	1.32M	1.36M	1,39M	1.39M
Foreign Workforce Growth	-	4.2%	2.6%	2.3%	0.4%
Total Workforce	3.4M	3.4M	3.5M	3.6M	3.7M
Workforce Growth	-	2.44%	2.53%	2.26%	1.72%
GDP Growth	1.3%	4.4%	2.9%	2.0%	2.0%
Productivity Growth	-0.5%	0.3%	-0.8%	-0.2%	1.0%

Source: Ministry of Manpower, Ministry of Trade and Industry

Prime Minister Lee's New Year message brought some good news on our productivity rates. In 2017, our productivity shot up to about 3 to 3.5 per cent and this is up from the minus 0.2 to 1 per cent in the recent past. Now, the questions that I personally have in my mind are: Is this growth going to be sustainable? How are our people doing as we lifted this productivity in 2017? Has our well-being as a people become better or worse? Have our people been working themselves to the bone to drive this productivity growth? Hence, the issue of job redesign becomes more and more important. We need to think about the job design carefully so that we can get the productivity lift that we want and still enable our people to be alright in terms of wellness, or else have other side effects like further aggravating our health care costs, which is already escalating. Total fertility rates may get affected and families may even fall apart because people are just too overworked.

When we think about productivity uplift, one of the first words that come to mind is, of course, technology. Now, in a physical space, there are heaps of machineries and robotics which you can consider to alleviate manual work.

In a cognitive space, we have things like machine learning and artificial intelligence (AI) which we could exploit.

Then there is also the agenda on skills. In recent years, Singapore has taken a Herculean effort to push for upskilling, reskilling and also lifelong learning. I personally have had the privilege of leading large consultancy engagements with SkillsFuture Singapore to develop skills framework for various industries. We want to future-proof our workforce, future-proof our economy. We want to boost social mobility and we obviously also want to boost workforce mobility. We also know that if we just look at technology and skills in isolation, we are looking at a picture that is incomplete. We need to relook at job design because the job design determines what work is to be done in a job and how the work is to be done. Without clarity on this, we will be ill-informed in terms of the most suitable technology enablement that we need to introduce into a job and the skills that are needed to operate the technology to do the work. If we introduce technology blindly into a job, productivity may in fact take a hit.

Job redesign is effectively the bridge between technology and skills. In reality, these three things are very tightly and closely interdependent. If we ask ten different people to give you their definitions of job redesign, do not be surprised to get eight or nine different answers. So, I thought it would be useful to propose a common definition for job redesign and job design so that we can have a common frame of mind as we discuss the topic today. Job design is simply a determination of what work should get done in a job and how that work is to be done. So, it is simply something that has a "what" component and a "how" component to it. Hence, job redesign is simply a relook at what work should get done in a job and how this work ought to be done. Now, it is not difficult to make a case for job redesign as an important national agenda going forward, but job redesign is not always easy to do.

Our economy is made up of organisations that are very different in terms of financial might and access to expertise. And there could be stark differences in terms of the scale of businesses and financial resources. Some understand job redesign better than others. Some organisations have internal organisation effectiveness functions with experts while some others do not have the same luxury. Organisations have different tolerance in terms of the time that they are prepared to wait before reaping the benefits of their job redesign investments. Some organisations are prepared to invest more and wait longer in order to see a greater impact. Some of these impacts can cut across jobs and functions and give you an enterprise-wide optimisation benefit. Some other organisations are quite impatient to see results and are prepared to accept that the impact will be a little bit more limited to single jobs or single functions. So, to drive this agenda at the national level, you will have to take these differences into consideration. There are also obstacles that stand in the way of a successful job redesign effort.

It is often difficult to choose the right unit of analysis. Do we design what work gets done or do we redesign how the work is to be done? Do we look at the responsibility blocks or the activities or clusters of those? If you look at process maps, you will find that it can exist at different levels of granularity. So, should we analyse level 1, level 2 or level 3 processes? It is also very challenging to predict a job before it even exists because we are modifying it along the way. This is especially so if making changes to a given job affects what and how adjacent jobs are to be done. Also related to this is the view that sometimes the long-term effects are different from the short-term effects of job redesign. Efficiency improves with time and practice, and if the incumbent is initially unfamiliar with the work environment, it may not allow the benefits of the job redesign effort to be obvious in the short term.

Another tricky matter is one of psychological security. We encourage organisations to closely involve the job incumbent in a job redesign effort. We do need to be very sensitive to the concerns that the incumbent may have. Our experience tells us that, especially for individuals in the Silver Age, when you mention the words "job redesign" to them, they get very nervous. They worry about whether it is an effort to remove them, they worry about whether life will get more difficult for them and they also potentially worry that you are attempting to redesign their job because you think that they are not performing well. So, we ought to be very sensitive to their sentiments.

There are also myths that need to be debunked about individuals in the Silver Age or those advancing into it. One common myth is one of declining ability to work in both the physical sense as well as the cognitive sense. Research by Oxford University Press breaks down cognitive ability into two components: fluid cognitive ability and crystallised cognitive ability. Fluid cognitive ability is involved in new learning or problem-solving performance and generally peaks somewhere in the 30s and then declines with age. Crystallised cognitive ability refers to intelligence gathered through knowledge and experience. There is evidence to suggest that individuals in the Silver Age are able to offset declines in fluid cognitive abilities with corresponding increase in knowledge and skills through accumulated experience.

So, how do we make job redesign really work? In 2016, we tested Mercer's job redesign architecture in an engagement with Singapore National Employers Federation (SNEF), where we deployed a job redesign toolkit targeting the retail, logistics, food and beverages (F&B) and hospitality industries. The intent was to make the workplace more age-inclusive in these industries. We tested this again in 2017 as part of an ongoing engagement with SPRING Singapore and Workforce Singapore. We developed job redesign solutions for a pilot group of seven retailers covering 36 jobs across all of the retail industries' sub-sectors and we drove the actual implementation of these solutions.

This architecture has several characteristics. It has a stratified "solutioning" model. This stratified model is meant to address the view that our economy is made up of organisations that have very different capabilities, financial might and appetite for job redesign investments.

First is what we call a "quick start". It is a simple do-it-yourself (DIY) guide. It is essentially a set of pre-packed solutions that organisations could deploy with little guidance on common issues faced. Now, the caveat here is that it may only enable you to get benefits that are localised in a single job, which may not be all that impactful. Second is a full methodology that is more elaborate; we call this "holistic". This may give you some enterprise-wide optimisation gains which are potentially very much more impactful. Third is what we call a "lite" version, the elaborateness of which is somewhere in between the two extremes. This may give you benefits across multiple jobs but limited to a single function. You can almost think of the "quick start" as a pharmacy which carries paracetamol, cough mixtures and band-aids to cope with common ailments that people face and want to self-medicate. This may give you a quick fix but may or may not address the root cause of your problem. The "lite" version is like seeing a general practitioner and the "holistic" version is like undergoing a major surgery. As you go from the "quick start" to the "holistic" model, the speed of implementation may come down as the complexity increases but the impact may get bigger. The effort may go up and the investment of resources may also correspondingly go up. We also need to anchor this on a set of real success stories. Essentially, we want to nudge more business owners to do job redesign, and we believe that the best way to do that is to have them know that their competition has done it and has done it successfully.

Being successful in job redesign is all about balance. There are different schools of thought. There is the Mechanistic Approach which is aimed at simplification, standardisation and repetition. The advantage of that is efficiency, easier staffing and reduced training. The disadvantage is decreased satisfaction and motivation. There is the Motivational Approach which is aimed at variety, autonomy, participation. The advantage of that is satisfaction and intrinsic motivation. The disadvantage is that of stress and errors. There are also other models. The key idea is to design a job that strikes a good balance and you get the benefits while avoiding the disadvantages. There are also common pitfalls to avoid in doing job redesign, and to be successful, we need to consciously avoid those.

Some very basic job redesign methods include uncoupling, unstacking and segmenting. As a result of these methods, the job could be enlarged, which is not a bad thing. It could be enriched, which is often a good thing. Or it could be reconfigured. There is also a risk that the job can get overloaded — and very often a bad thing. There could also be tasks that fall through the cracks and are left unperformed. The job could also get impoverished which is something that we want to avoid.

We believe that to make job redesign truly work, we need to take a step back and look at the bigger picture. We know that at the core and centre of it, the intent is to bring about a sustained gainful employment of our Silver Age population. Job redesign is just a means that is aimed at lowering the demands of the job to commensurate with the cognitive, sensory and motor abilities of the Silver Age. It is also about job fulfilment. But we are also very circumspect; we understand that, ultimately, we need the business owners to invest in job redesign. We need strong business cases to convince them to do a few things. Essentially, we need them to start and continue employing Silver Age workers and investing in job redesign initiatives and age-inclusive practices. For them to be convinced, they need to believe that they can get better commercial gains and business results from heightened work performance from the Silver Age. As a result of the high performance, they get strong business results due to job redesign. And for the Silver Age workers to elevate and sustain performance, they need continual training and mentoring because job redesign is unlikely to be a one-off effort. We might have done a successful job to really design a particular piece of work before but as business needs change, the job demands may also evolve and hence we need continual coaching, mentoring and training. Very importantly, as our workforce becomes increasingly multi-generational in nature, employees need to establish practices that enable the different generations to not only tolerate each other but instead to enjoy working with each other. As you can see, this is a circular issue that is quite often the critical point of entry to nudge business owners to take a leap of faith.

II

The Singapore Community: Solidarity not Contention

CHAPTER 3

The Future Politics of Ageing

CHAN HENG CHEE

The ageing population is undeniably one of the major issues of our time. It is inevitable and will happen in all societies globally. Demographic trends have the quality of certainty, short of dramatic change due to war or a catastrophic disaster. No one has denied population ageing. The other issue of our time is climate change but there are some who deny it. A common concern for most countries is that as the population grows older, there may be emerging conflicts in society between the population who are growing older and the working age population which is not growing commensurately. We frequently highlight the uncomfortable truth that the old age dependency ratio will rise. There will be far more dependent people then there are working people. The *IPS Background Paper* has projected this. Christopher Gee has pointed out that the dependency ratio will be 24 older people per 100 persons of working age in 2020 and 54 older people per 100 persons of working age in 2040. Now, contrast this with 8 older aged persons per 100 working age persons in 1980 and 11 to a 100 in 2000. The burden is great, but is it just about who pays the taxes, who pays the bills and who gets what space?

Sociologists and gerontologists write about generational wars or age wars and age conflicts. Generational conflict sounds familiar but generational war and age war seem overstated. The only age war I can think of — if it is one — is the conflict in the United States over the Vietnam War on the rights and wrongs of the war between young men — many college students who were drafted to fight and die in a country far away — and middle-aged older politicians and generals who were making decisions about the war. As some of you remember, protests spread across the campuses and industries. The Vietnam War triggered the counter-culture revolution in America in the 1960s and a major "value disruption" with it. By the time they realised that it was about "values-change", all ages were pulled in. Young people did start the process but it became intergenerational. One can also think of young Chinese students in Tiananmen protesting against the economic and political issues of the day against the central authorities. It had nothing to do with age conflict; it was a protest against the Communist Party and government on issues of inflation, unemployment and corruption. The Arab Spring, which has been associated with young people did not only involve young people, it involved older people too. In the end, the protests included everyone and they were not about age-related issues.

Now, if generational wars and age wars sound far-fetched, generational conflict and tensions do exist in Asia as well as in the West. Lester Thurow, the late political economist and Dean of the Massachusetts Institute of Technology (MIT), Sloan School, went so far as to say in 1996, that in the years ahead, class warfare is apt to be redefined as the young against the old rather than the rich against the poor because of the explosion of public pension costs and healthcare. His prediction has not come true — in the 20 years since he made the statement — in the United States, in Europe or elsewhere. In Asia, culture, tradition and context will play a role in shaping the acceptance of burdens and the allocation of resources.

So, what will happen to our politics in the coming decades, given the growing senior vote? How will Singaporeans react to the claims of an ageing society? What will happen to the politics of integration as it pertains to allocation and redistribution? Integration in ageing societies inevitably raises the question of immigration.

Let me talk about allocation and redistribution first. I have commented before that we do not have the same resistance to the allocation of budget monies to subsidies for the old, the disabled, the poor and single mothers with children that you will find in some industrialised societies. There, it is an ideological issue because Republicans in the United States and the Conservative Party in the United Kingdom may not support welfare subsidies for those who cannot support themselves. There is usually a huge debate. In Singapore, it is different. If anything, Singaporeans applaud moves to increase welfare payments to the needy and say that the government should give more. But of course, the government has not really raised taxes yet to pay for the subsidies though they talk about it. Our attitude can partly be explained by the exposure to the many years of early PAP's democratic socialism. We have been socialised into a sense of egalitarianism and a sense of the larger good.

I read a post recently by Dave Chew of Singapore. It was in Quora[1]. I quote him because he reflects the public sentiment. He was answering the question, "Do Singaporeans still favour the PAP?" and this is what Dave Chew wrote and I quote, "The Singapore electorate is probably conservative financially, centrist in politics, pragmatic and not so idealistic. We are altruistic and believe in equality but pragmatism is more important to us. We have little interest in the highfalutin ideals of freedom of speech, of human rights in the Western sense. We prefer to gauge our lawmakers by real changes they make to our lives. We are not stuck-up by the Left or Right battles, and what we are keen on is to see our fellow citizens having a better life. If it means more subsidies, we're cool. If it means more taxes, which happened in GE2015, it normally goes without so much as a whimper. Fundamentally, it is about what works and not about what should. Dave Chew went on to discuss "Yes, we support the PAP but...!" So, he is not a flag waver. It is interesting that he makes this comment. I ask, "Will Singapore's tolerance for tax increases remain?"

Healthcare costs are indeed rising rapidly. The topmost line is the United States in purple. The thick orange line represents Singapore and only South Korea is rising less than Singapore. So, while compared to other OECD countries, our healthcare costs are not as high. There is no doubt they are going northwards.

---

[1] Quora is a question-and-answer website where questions are asked, answered, edited and organised by its community of users.

Healthcare Expenditure Per Capita, $US

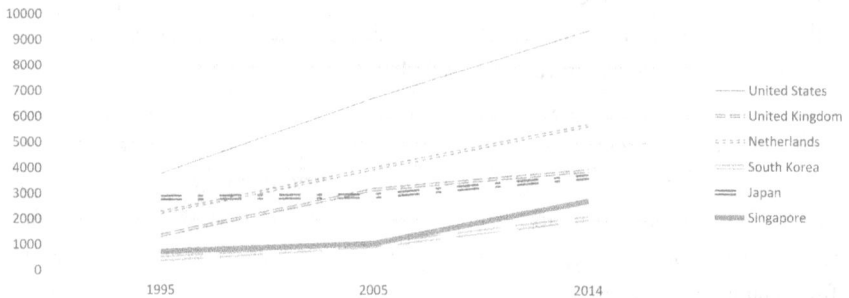

Total Healthcare Expenditure, % of GDP	Country	1995	2005	2014
	United States	13.09%	15.15%	17.14%
	United Kingdom	6.69%	8.24%	9.12%
	Netherlands	7.44%	9.60%	10.90%
	South Korea	3.67%	5.33%	7.37%
	Japan	6.62%	8.18%	10.23%
	Singapore	2.94%	3.74%	4.92%

Source: World Bank

We can have smart policies to try to moderate costs, but in the end, with the projected figure of 900,000 seniors aged 65 and above in 2030 — which is only 12 years away — and the numbers will increase as we live longer and have better health — health costs will be hefty.

I believe if taxes continue to increase, there will be unhappiness as per what the IPS survey shows, although there is a large group of neutrals at this point. Will this result in younger Singaporeans demanding a reduction in older citizens' benefits? I am sure there is a tipping point but we are not there yet, judging by the political debate. There is the matter of public policy choices about what proportion of the budget should be allocated to the expenditure for the young and for the older citizens before there is a contestation. I do not think we have that argument yet. Today, we have simple conflicts of interests between bicyclists and users of personal mobility devices (PMD) — usually younger people — using the walkways reserved for the senior citizens in the housing estates. It is a contestation over space.

Now, some have argued that what may temper opposition to these allocations is the reality that everyone will age, and the expectation of the below 65 that one day, they too will benefit from the same subsidies. This casts a different light on things. When the Pioneer Generation Package

(PGP) was offered, not only were the Pioneers made a happy lot, their children were happy too because the healthcare costs for the family were lightened. But will there be pressure from those who just missed the package?

As Singaporeans live longer, it is not only healthcare costs that will be a political issue, there could be conflict or tensions over jobs and power positions. Today, we find that older persons do not do well in finding the appropriate kind of work. 25.8 per cent of elderly residents are in the labour force. Where are senior Singaporeans working? Which areas? Cleaners, labourers and related workers form the largest group. The number of older services and sales workers, legislators, senior officials and managers is declining but the professionals are keeping up. The number of older clerical support workers is also growing.

Percentage of Elderly in various occupations (1990-2015)

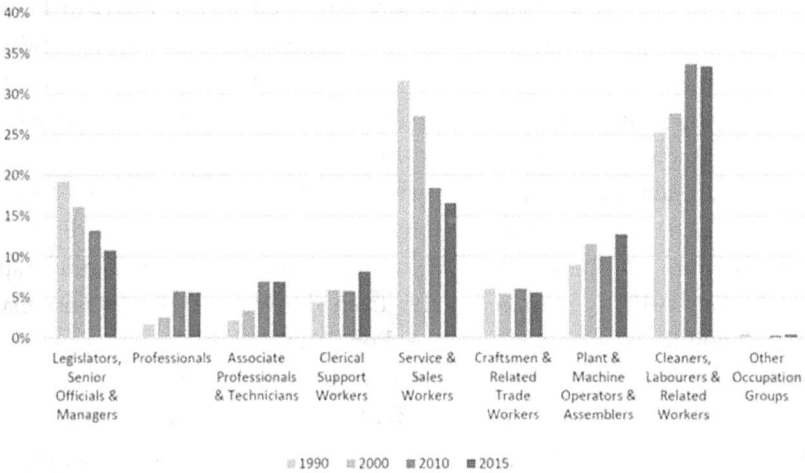

1990 2000 2010 2015

Source: Department of Statistics

The senior citizens that are growing older are better educated, even as they age, and they may want to hold on to their last jobs or aspire to a better job. Some countries such as the United Kingdom do not have a retirement age at all.

I was told by a young colleague at my Centre that she would resent it if she were told she should give up her job simply because she reached a determined number like 65 or 67 if she were still mentally or physically capable to hold the job. That would be "ageism" — bear in mind that there is the enabling technology to help the older workers. At the same time, I think we have to be aware that increased automation will do away with many jobs. The problem for us in Singapore, as in most societies, is to find the sweet spot — the jobs for seniors that have to be created now that some jobs are taken away. Where do they fit?

Next question: the next generation will be impatient, waiting to take over positions at the top or near the top. How does society deal with these pressures? I believe there will be tensions. In Singapore, we have a tradition of circulation at the highest echelons of the Civil Service. No Permanent Secretary gets more than ten years as "Perm Sec". In politics, we are also pushing the circulation of leaders. We have the fourth generation now, and I read that the Workers Party will be changing leaders too. Will we see a group of "grey panthers" emerging, fighting to hold their place in society and the economy? Will they demand more job opportunities and the right kind of jobs? Do they have to fight against "ageism"? I saw many American corporate leaders keeping very fit. They made sure they went to the gym, looked fit and good so that their younger colleagues would not be able to push them aside. So, please keep fit. Look good!

Looking ahead, the "grey vote" will be a substantial constituency. In 2030, it is projected that 900,000 persons will be 65 and above. In 2030, the population of Singapore citizens, if you hold that there will be no immigration at all from 2013 — I am taking this from the White Paper (A Sustainable Population for a Dynamic Singapore: Population White Paper) — will be 3.4 million. With 900,000 aged 65 and above, in a population of 3.4 million, that makes your vote about 24 to 26 per cent. So, it is a substantial vote. For the PAP, it has been something of a vote bank. In recent years though, because of job disruption, some in their mid-50s and mid-60s may be more disgruntled. Inflation and the inability of pensioners or retirees to make ends meet is an effective slogan to rally votes in any country. It is also true that among the high-income groups in many countries, Singapore included, older citizens form a substantial proportion. Amongst the rich, there are also the old — you'll get there too. The aged do not form a monolithic vote. In Singapore, ethnicity and religion will further impact on voting behaviour, depending on the issues of the day, and it need not be just age-related.

There are two other issues concerning age integration that I would like to highlight. I speak of age harassment. While there may not be public conflict or protests against the ageing population, age harassment takes place. Not the "hashtag me-too" (#MeToo) harassment but the abuse of the elderly in the homes by family members unable to cope with an ageing relative who is bedridden and hard to care for. There could also be poor treatment in ill-run institutions. Government and society need to find ways to alleviate stress in the family and monitor institutions for the aged. Laurence Lien will tell you about that. Now, I mentioned "ageism" earlier. What is "ageism"? It is prejudice and discrimination on the grounds of a person's age — most frequently seen in employment. This is an issue everywhere, and in Singapore, though there are some exceptions made to the possession of special skills. You can say that those who are older can be innovative as well. I will say, "Yes they are very innovative." In a situation of declining population, this ought to be less of an issue but change in the mindset does not happen automatically.

A tight labour force can help too. The re-employment age in Singapore has been raised in 2017 from 65 to 67 for eligible employees. This is a good step but there must be job growth for this to work well. You just cannot say "hire the older people". There must be job growth and there needs to be genuine rethinking on the concept of ageing and viewing the elderly people as an asset rather than liability.

Now, let me talk about immigration, regeneration and renewal. How can ageing societies cope with renewal or regeneration? Anti-immigration is a global sentiment. Singapore is not like every society and every country; we are a city and we are a city-state. This debate will be continuing and the future debate could be contentious, but as a city-state, our working population cannot be replenished by internal migration. In other countries like Indonesia and China, people from the rural areas come to the city to work. Inevitably, immigration therefore comes up as a partial solution to augmenting population numbers and the workforce. Pro-birth policies are the other measure but there are limits to their success. If Singapore turns off the immigration tap altogether and does not take in any new foreign non-residents, the Singapore population is expected to start shrinking in 2025 — seven years away.

Japan, it has been discussed, which has a population of a 127 million today, will shrink to 50 million by 2100 if they do nothing. The Japanese government has been slowly but surely turning to immigration to deal with a population decline, though they are a long way off. Foreigners constituted only 1.8 per cent of their population in 2016. Some say Japan has robots, they produce robots to step up productivity. But what is a population of robots? There is no soul to the nation. Immigration is deeply unpopular in Japan, and Japan is homogeneous and generally closed society.

Like it or not, the issue of immigration must be addressed in Singapore. The conversation, I think, has shifted a little. Singaporeans generally accept that some immigration is necessary. They realise that older citizens and young children need caregivers, which the working family cannot provide adequately. But they would like sustainable immigration and would like to be assured that their core identity will not be eroded. Singaporeans are most concerned about job security. It is an issue then of moderated immigration. The issue is not immigration or no immigration. We have gone past that! The question is how many and what types of immigration? We need the creative and the innovators, as well as caregivers and unskilled workers. As I said, there has to be job growth. Philip Yeo, in his interview with Sumiko Tan, said, "We don't want so many masseurs, we want people who can come in and also create jobs, the innovators."

Now, when the numbers shrink drastically and the economy and society is affected, I think Singaporeans will be pragmatic. The critical issue is how we will integrate new citizens and how we can integrate them better.

Fortunately, we are not the first ageing society in the world. We can learn from the example of others.

CHAPTER 4

Creating a Golden Age for Ageing: Opportunities We are Missing

LAURENCE LIEN

Looking 30 years forward, my children will be around my age now. Their children would be young. I do not want to be a burden to them. I want to be independent, so I need to look at what life will be like if I want to be independent. In terms of the end of life, there are four main scenarios: sudden death, terminal illness, frailty and organ failure. Organ failure is usually associated with losing functionality and chronic illness. Experiencing frailty is also a slow decline towards death. With a terminal illness, it is a relatively quick but painful decline, while sudden death is immediate.

Proposed Trajectories of Dying

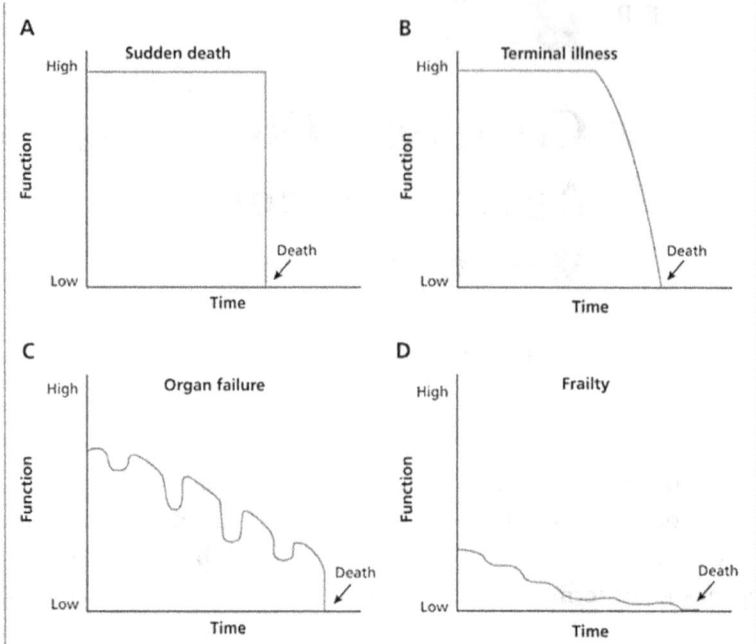

Source: Lunney, J. R., Lynn, J., & Hogan, C. (2002). Profiles of older Medicare decedents. *Journal of American Geriatric Society*, 50: 1109.

When faced with terminal illness, it is important to reduce futile end-of-life (EoL) treatments, of which there is too much. In fighting chronic disease, we should focus on preventative care. In my view, there are too many people in Singapore who are chronically sick and frail, and there is too much organ failure. Thankfully, the kidney disease numbers have improved for the first time in decades. A chief executive officer of an Australian nursing home operator came to visit our nursing homes. I asked him about his first impression of nursing homes in Singapore and to highlight differences from those in Australia. He said, "Too many wheelchairs! Why are there so many wheelchairs in your nursing homes? We don't see so many in ours. People are more independent and the age profile is a lot older." We are not keeping people well enough and we are also not tackling end-of-life care well.

In Being Mortal, Atul Gawande says that fewer than one third of patients with an end-stage diagnosis discuss their goals and preferences with the clinicians when they come closer to the end of life. We are wasting too many resources on futile care. Gawande's Ariadne Lab came up with the serious illness conversation card. Such conversations almost never happen in Singapore. The focus is on allowing people to talk about what is most important when they are at the end-of-life and to avoid what is happening today. Seventy-seven per cent of Singaporeans want to die at home, yet only 27 per cent do so. Sixty-one per cent die in hospitals.

Ageism is also something omnipresent in the context of employment, the media, the roads, public transport, at home, in the community, advertisements, popular culture, shops that always cater for the younger set, and even casual conversations. Ageism is pervasive and it is self-fulfilling. If there is a universal belief that older people are a burden, they will quickly become a burden and that turns into a fact of life. Instead, we need to see the glass as half-full rather than half-empty. We focus so much on what we lose in old age when there is so much that we still have; in fact, what we still have is still growing. As a result, we are missing a lot of opportunities because we do not see older persons as being able to contribute to our society and being able to live with purpose.

Age is a self-fulfilling prophecy. Some researchers found that seniors with more positive self-perceptions of ageing, which is measured up to 23 years earlier, live seven and a half years more than those who have less positive self-perceptions of ageing. This advantage remained after accounting for differences in gender, socio-economic status, loneliness, functional status and so on. Many other studies show that as we become older, we become happier. Our ability to handle stress improves, we savour our relationships, we live life with more authenticity, we are better at emotional regulation, become more grateful and people develop the intrinsic urge to give back.

The concept of declining fluid cognitive ability as you grow older suggests that you cannot learn new things or problem-solve over time. Another more optimistic study shows that as you grow older, you become more distracted. Your cognitive control worsens and if you perform tasks that need focused attention, obviously your performance declines with lower cognitive control. However, if you focus on tasks that benefit from diffused attention, your performance heightens. In short, if you are more distracted, you are better at creative problem-solving and taking in new information.

We often use 65 years as a cut-off point for retirement, dependency and so on. Instead, we should shift the benchmark of 65 years because the 70-year-old in 2014 is behaving like a 65-year-old in 1999. In terms of the labour force participation rate, those above 70 accounted for 15.3 per cent of the labour force in 2014. That is even higher than the labour force participation rate in 1999 of those aged 65 years and above. Health-adjusted life expectancy at birth has increased about four years for both males and females. The old-age dependency ratio in 1999 — using the benchmark of 65 years — was 10.8 per cent. In contrast, the old-age dependency ratio in 2014 using the benchmark of 70 years was 9.9 per cent. This is an improvement. Seventy could be the "new" 65, but there will be oncoming issues.

Old age dependency ratio actually improved if 70 is the new 65!

	1999	2014
Life Expectancy at birth	77.6	82.6
Labour Force Participation Rate		
65 Years & Over	12.4%	25.2%
70 Years & Over	7.6%	15.3%
Health-Adjusted Life Expectancy at Birth		
Male	68	72
Female	71	75
Old Age Dependency Ratio		
65 Years & Over (per 100 aged 20-64)	10.8%	16.7%
70 Years & Over (per 100 aged 20-70)	6.5%	9.9%

Source: Department of Statistics, Ministry of Manpower, Estimates from Lancet data for 1990, 2006 and 2016

We should play, work and learn throughout our lives. But what jobs allow us to do this? I challenge employers. If the jobs for the middle-aged cannot allow them to live life in parallel today, then there is no chance for older people to work while enjoying life in the future.

Actress Jane Fonda is an amazing "age advocate" and she made a fantastic observation that one should not see "age as pathology" but "age as a potential". Basically, if we think about age while focusing on physical elements, then it is an arch because there is a decline. But if you think about age as moving towards authenticity, happiness and wisdom, then it is a staircase all the way to the end.

Here are some examples of how we can integrate the optimism, contributions and strengths of older people into society. One example is the "Ibasho" in Japan, started by Dr Emi Kiyota, an environmental gerontologist. It has been applied in Nepal and the Philippines. "Ibasho" means a place where you can feel like yourself. There are very few places in Singapore where older people can feel like themselves — where they do not lose respect from others in society, where they are with others and are contributing. In an "Ibasho," the older people serve drinks and snacks. The important thing is that they are valuable assets to the community. They have a voice and together with the facilitators, develop these projects. They become change agents and they care for other people instead of just being cared for.

I have, in my time, been focusing on developing assisted living facilities in Singapore. Assisted living is very different from nursing homes, and is usually for those who do not have severe care needs in terms of help with activities of daily living (ADLs). There is a sense of community and everyone contributes to the life of the place. Key considerations when designing an assisted living facility include respect for residents of nursing homes as those who can exercise choices and be empowered to do things for themselves and for other people.

The main problem with older people is not even finances or the physical self. It is loneliness. There is a need to build up the social capital of older people. First, among themselves. There is so much potential for mutual help and self-help. Second, with younger people. The fear that there will be a constant contestation over things like space is because younger people and older people do not come together to problem-solve. When they are able to do that, they offer solutions, not just to the problems inherent in ageing, but also to an array of other challenges that demand attention. So, when a senior mentors a youth, for example, it is a cure for loneliness for the older person and there is also guidance for the young. Age-friendly infrastructure can also be child-friendly infrastructure. We should not just focus on solutions for older people.

Older people are consumers too. We forget about that and we never advertise with them in mind or create enough products for them. "Genki Kaki" is an initiative of the Lien Foundation. We brought two older people to Japan to test out their eldercare facilities and to go to their malls, which cater to older people. So, we brought them to this mall where older people start their day by having exercises. The whole complex is geared towards them. It is so welcoming and of course, the two from Singapore said, "Would it not be nice if we had something like this at home?" The silver industry is a huge opportunity and if Singapore is an ageing population, we should be at the centre of this for the rest of the region.

We have also experimented with "Gym Tonic" — gyms for the older people using pneumatic exercise equipment. HUR is a supplier of incredible state-of-the-art exercise equipment from Finland. A radio frequency identification device (RFID) recognises the wearer and adjusts the weights according to what his or her physiotherapist has prescribed. With enough repetitions over time, the therapist can programme the equipment to automatically adjust the weights. We have been implementing this in many institutions. We have rolled this out for the community to fight frailty. This is very important because once you start being frail everything steadily goes downhill.

One of the things that we are building together with Khoo Chwee Neo Foundation and Peacehaven Nursing Home is the project "Jade Circle", which is part of Peacehaven. This is a nursing home concept, different from assisted living, but we are trying to transform it. On the inside there will be a cafe and a hairdresser. There will also be a mini-supermarket which is safe for even those who have dementia. All these will allow the residents go through the same routine that they have always done.

In short, we must change mindsets. This is critical. We must maintain optimism, act with urgency, and prototype quickly with seniors as part of the solution. We should not just do things for them. They must be part of the solution. Unlike race or religion which cannot be changed, we all will age. So, if we think long-term, we are doing things for ourselves and for the future. We will not do something that does not benefit the whole society overall. With this, we can create that "Golden Age of Ageing", the vision that I started with.

Lunch Dialogue

CHAPTER 5

Ageing with Vigour

TEO CHEE HEAN

We are now living much longer than before. In the 1950s, the expected lifespan was around 61 years. Today, those who are aged around 65 can expect to live another 21 years. These additional years of life are really a bonus, received from the investments that we have made in sanitation, healthcare, good housing and a good clean, safe and secure living environment. Children born today can expect to live up to around 83 years old. With improvements in biomedical sciences, we can only guess how many more bonus years today's children might have by the time they are in their 60s or 70s. Greater longevity is a bonus if we are well prepared for it. We can age with vigour if each one of us prepares himself or herself well, if we prepare ourselves well in our communities, and if all of us together, as a nation, are well prepared.

We are entering a phase where the number of seniors is increasing rapidly. The baby boomers are coming into their senior years. Today, we have about 500,000 seniors aged 65 and above. By 2030, this will double to around 900,000. The number of citizens aged 80 and above will also more than double from around 100,000 today to around 200,000 by 2030. In fact, our citizens aged 80 and above are one of the fastest-growing segments of our population. Baby boomers were born in fairly large cohorts of 50,000 to 60,000 whereas the cohorts today are almost half that, around 32,000 births a year, even though in the last three to four years we have had a higher number of marriage and births among citizens than we have had in the previous decade. The United Nations (UN) has described population ageing as one of the defining features of our times. Countries are seeing populations age at an unprecedented rate and the level of ageing will differ from country to country.

In Singapore, today, they are about 4.4 adults aged 20 to 64 (what we would conventionally call "working age") to every senior aged 65 and above. In Europe, it is about 3.0, and Japan, 2.0. Singapore will hit Europe's current levels of ageing by around 2020 and Japan's current levels by around 2040. We are also ageing much more rapidly than other countries. It took France over 100 years to transit from an ageing society, which by some demographers' definition is 7 per cent of the population, to an aged society with 14 per cent of the population aged 65 and over. It has taken us only 19 years and we crossed that mark last year. On the positive side, we are actually much better prepared than others.

The need to prepare for an ageing population could already be seen by the mid-1980s. Life expectancy was increasing and the baby boomers had already been born. However, in the mid-1980s, many people might not have been ready to think that far ahead and contemplate the range of measures that were needed to deal with this situation. Nevertheless, we were able to take several measures early, to set in place resilient institutions that are built on strong foundations and principles. These have now put us in a better position to look after ourselves and as a society as we age.

Now, one such pillar is the Central Provident Fund (CPF), which helps Singaporeans to save for their old age, cover medical expenses and purchase basic health insurance. This is a fully funded system and will be sustainable for generations to come. This is a fundamental difference and a fundamental strength. In many other countries, pension promises are not fully funded and pension payments have to be met from current government budgets, placing a great strain on the current working generation. The CPF system, as it was operating, was not good enough and it was improved significantly in 2009, with the introduction of CPF Life. CPF Life provides lifelong pay-outs for future cohorts of seniors by pooling together our longevity risk. In this way, our seniors are assured of monthly payments for as long as they live, compared to the previous CPF system, where seniors got a fixed amount but risked living beyond the time when their own CPF retirement accounts ran out. That is a very frightening position to be in and CPF Life deals with that problem. For those unable to save enough by themselves, we have targeted assistance through housing grants, Workfare and Silver Support.

As for healthcare, we have MediShield Life today, which provides lifelong universal health insurance coverage for all. Introduced in 2015, MediShield

Life made a significant improvement over the earlier MediShield, which only provided health insurance coverage up to the age of 92 on an opt-out basis. MediShield also did not cover pre-existing conditions. So MediShield Life deals with these three fundamental shortcomings of the old MediShield. MediShield Life now means that seniors need not worry about not qualifying for health insurance due to pre-existing conditions, or again living beyond the age when they can get health insurance. With MediShield Life and CPF Life, living longer is a blessing. The introduction of CPF Life and MediShield Life are therefore game changers. These national, social risk-pooling schemes mean that to a larger extent than before, we are all helping one another to cope better together with the uncertainties associated with ageing. So, with this national risk pooling, we are not facing ageing alone.

We are facing ageing together and we pool our risk of longevity together. Our healthcare expenditure to look after our seniors actually comes from three sources: sharing risk collectively through MediShield Life, our own Medisave accounts and cash payments, and also very significant subsidies from the government to hospitals and polyclinics for subsidised healthcare such as in our B2 and C wards. The doubling of our population of seniors by 2030 means that the subsidies that we provide from our government budget for healthcare will grow very substantially. Even if we assume that doctors and nurses have no more pay rises in the coming years and if our medical system uses exactly the same drugs and operates with exactly the same costs as today, just the doubling of the seniors means that the resources needed to support healthcare system from our budget will increase dramatically.

Today, the largest expenditure item in our government budget is defence, followed by education and health. Health today is around 2.4 per cent of gross domestic product (GDP). This is already a significant increase from 2007 when health was just around 0.8 per cent of GDP. That was when there were about 300,000 Singaporeans over the age of 65. Today, we have about 500,000 and by 2030 we will have 900,000 over the age of 65. So as a percentage of GDP, this is a three-fold increase in expenditure from the government budget and we could expect that health expenditure may overtake education in our government budget in the coming years. We will have to make sure that our budget remains on a sound footing so that we have the resources to take care of our seniors as they age and to make sure that we help our children take care of us. These measures, like CPF Life,

MediShield Life and a sound government budget sufficient to fund our current health care needs, have put us on a firmer footing than many other countries. We still need to be careful so that we maintain that sound foundation, those sound principles that have given us this firm footing as we develop policies for the future. Our past generations have given us these "bonus years", which I and those in my generation enjoy. It places all of us as a nation on a firmer footing to age with confidence and vigour. We must also continue to build on this for future generations. I think that it is our responsibility.

I have just outlined what all of us can do together at a national level but we also have to take ownership for what we can do collectively in our communities and what we can do as individuals to support our families and ourselves to age with vigour. It is not just something for the government to do or something for the government to take care of. We need to do it as a community, we need to do it ourselves and in our families. As a community, we can all play our part to enable our seniors to embrace the opportunities that come from longevity and live life to the fullest. For example, we have initiatives to enable those who want to work, to stay in work longer. We raised the re-employment age from 65 to 67 from July last year. Alongside this, we have introduced a special employment credit that helps companies to pay part of the wages of workers aged 55 and above, earning up to $4,000 a month. This today benefits about 340,000 workers and helps us to achieve a high rate of employment of workers between the ages 55 and 64. We are round about 67.3 per cent right now. This is comparable to the levels in Germany and Denmark, but I think we can still do better.

There are also grants to enable our companies to redesign workplaces and jobs — but these grants and credits are meaningful only when employers value and tap on the experience and skills that seniors can offer. Our seniors too have to do their part to keep up with the new skills that are required in the workplace. They need to make themselves relevant, useful and value adding. SkillsFuture and other programmes are targeted at this and we can also redesign jobs to have more flexible work arrangements so that there is part-time work, job sharing and working from home. Technology offers so much more opportunity. The gig economy, often talked of as something for millennials, is not just for the millennials. If we redesign jobs to be more flexible, seniors are one of the largest groups that can take part in this gig economy as well. So, only through a changed mind-set and a concerted effort, can we help make it possible for seniors to remain in the workforce for as long as they are able and willing to do so.

I visited Changi Airport and SATS recently. I met Dolly. Dolly is an automated, guided vehicle for food delivery. Workers no longer have to push heavy trolleys, weighing up to 200 kilogrammes. The Singapore Public Service is also doing its part. As at December 2016, we had close to 3,000 public officers now aged 65 and above. This is up from 500 in 2010. These officers continue to contribute well. In fact, our longest-serving public officer, Mr Puteh Bin Mahamood from the Elections Department, is 84 years old and first joined 70 years ago in 1947.

Within our communities, there is also much that we can do to build community spirit and look out for one another. The Japanese are very good at this. Japan is well known for having very strong community-based support. These younger seniors in the Nippon Active Life Club in Osaka helped to take care of senior-seniors enabling them to continue to live in their own homes, instead of moving to assisted care facilities. These younger seniors are "paying it forward". We can always stay young at heart, keep ourselves active and vigorous and encourage others to join in and do so too. One of my Pasir Ris residents, Uncle Chong, is 90 years old and continues to conduct weekly swimming lessons for other seniors, encouraging them to remain active and fit even in their advanced years. Another older lady in my constituency used to run the canteen when Changi Airport was being built and she cooked single-handedly. They remain active and support each other.

In 2016, we started the Community Networks for Seniors (CNS), to develop strong community-based support to complement family support. The community network reaches out to seniors to support them to age well in place. So CNS coordinates the efforts of government agencies, VWOs (Voluntary Welfare Organisations) and grassroots organisations to bring senior-centric programmes and services to their doorstep. Volunteers such as our pioneer generation ambassadors and grassroots leaders encourage our seniors to attend health screening and talks as well as exercises and social interest groups. We are also matching seniors living alone with befrienders and neighbours who can help them. Seniors living alone is another rapidly growing segment of our population. The goal is to build a close-knit community in our neighbourhoods where seniors can age happily, healthily and actively in place. To promote intergenerational bonding, we are also co-locating childcare and elder care facilities. The first such site is at Kampung Admiralty where a childcare centre and active ageing hub are located side-by-side. Over the next 10 years, we will extend this to some 10 new Housing and Development Board (HDB) housing precincts.

Finally, as individuals and as families, we also have to do our part to support our senior family members to age well and enjoy their silver years. The warm embrace of families plays an important role to provide meaning to life, support, mutual love and care. The government recognises this and, in fact, our policies are designed to encourage family members to help one another and to live close to another. We encourage children to live together or close together with their parents by giving priority for housing and grants. We have special incentives to encourage individuals to top-up the CPF accounts of loved ones.

Our tax policy encourages intergenerational support in terms of parent and grandparent caregiver reliefs. In addition, we need to rethink our own individual approach to life in ageing, so that we can all lead long, happy, healthy and purposeful lives. We can do this with lifelong learning, acquisition of new skills, keeping active through work and exercise, finding meaning through community and voluntary work and fulfilment with our families. Living longer does not mean being old for longer but means staying young for longer. So, we need to keep fit, keep learning and keep contributing. When I was 29, 30 years old, I thought that if I can keep running and jogging when I am in the 50s that would be fine. Today, I am in my 60s and I can still do it and I hope to continue doing it for as long as possible. It is the approach and attitude that we take towards ageing. So, instead of merely adding years to life, we should be adding life to years.

We do need a mind-set change in the way we think about ageing and stand the whole way we think about ageing on its head. We need a collective commitment at all levels. What can I in my family do? What can we do in our communities and workplaces? What can we all do together as a nation to prepare ourselves? Our pioneers laid a strong foundation for us. Each one of us and our families, businesses, employers, our community, need to shift toward a notion of ageing with vigour. To live a full life and life to the full and create a vibrant and vigorous Singapore for all ages.

III

Singaporeans
Living Longer: Asset or
Liability?

CHAPTER 6

Longevity and Social Welfare in Singapore

DAVID CANNING

I started out my academic career as a game theorist, working on issues of rationality and human behaviour. In my 30s, I attended a talk, at a session very much like this one, where I heard someone speak, and what they said changed my life. What they said was, "The big question in the world is why some countries are rich and some countries are poor. It is the enormous income gaps between countries that is really the big question in economics, and that is the thing we have to understand." That led me to study economic development and do empirical work. About 20 years ago, I worked with a colleague, David Bloom. We worked on a book about the "Asian economic miracle", and the question there was "Why was Asia so successful?" How has Asia, in one generation, gone from extreme poverty to wealth? The answer we found empirically was that it was fundamentally caused by two things: one is health. Improvements, particularly in children's health, led to better cognitive and physical development. Second, demographics are heading towards low fertility, more female labour market participation and more investment in children. These are the two key drivers of the economic take-off.

When we first came up with the term "demographic dividend" and we went to the World Bank and talked about it, people laughed and said that this was just an association and it was not causality. I think my academic career since then has been focussed on proving that these mechanisms are real and causal. If there are any investors in the room, I would like to say that I have just come here from Tanzania and I think Africa is now poised for take-off.

It is poised for a "demographic dividend". There have been enormous health improvements in children, fertility is falling and women with high school education in Africa are now at replacement fertility. You do not see it yet in the macroeconomic data but you see it at the household level. I think Africa is now exactly where Asia was in the 1970s and 80s.

However, this conference is really about the other end of the demographic transition. This conference is about ageing. I would say that there is an unfortunate definitional issue about dependency rates. I think children are dependent, someone must look after them, but I think calling old people dependent is really a mistake. They can be dependent. You can organise your society so that the old are dependent, but you do not have to. If people save for retirement and have their own resources, there is no need to think of them as a dependent. In fact, the other big cause of the Asian economic miracle was savings and investment. Those savings were generated by people saving for retirement. Saving for retirement is another incredibly important source of economic growth, and so, I think it is a mistake to think of the elderly as a dependent. A point I want to make — and I think it is a point that we should emphasise — is that longer healthy lifespans are an enormous gain in terms of human welfare. Living longer, and a particularly key point here, is about living a longer healthy life. The onset of physical and mental disability is going up faster than lifespans. We are seeing a compression of the period at the end of life where people are too ill to take care of themselves.

So, we have this enormous gain, enormous improvement in human welfare, and the question then is why do we have to have a conference? Why do we not just have a celebration? But we are not just celebrating, we are having these meetings and saying, "Well, this is a problem." And why is it a problem? It is because it is inconsistent with our current institutional arrangements. The fact that we are living longer healthy lives is not consistent with the way most countries have set up their institutions. To me, the very simple answer is that institutions have to change. In many countries, there is a wish, in a sense, a desire or a hope that this problem goes away. People want to keep their existing institutions and not have to deal with the elderly. I think that is completely the wrong approach. Institutions have to change in society. I would say that Singapore is much better set up to deal with this issue than most countries. I think that many countries have locked themselves into "pay-as-you-go" systems and transfer systems that make the old dependent, and are having to live with the consequences of that. Singapore has had a lot of foresight in terms of policy and has not done what some of these other countries have done. So, institutions, not people, have to change. When I say institutions, it is not just government, it includes families, communities, employers and civil society.

Another point concerns incentives. A lot of what goes on in society is about social norms and social relationships much more than incentives, and relying entirely on incentives is not going to get us to the right answer. The way we think and talk about things is incredibly important. So, one thing I want to try to have you take away is a new way of thinking. One of the institutions that we are mentally locked into is maximising GDP or GDP per capita. We have this very measurable concept. What I see around the world is that GDP growth is going to slow down because of population ageing and people see that as an enormous problem. The purpose of human life is not to maximise GDP. The purpose of GDP is to maximise human welfare and the way we live our lives. You have got it completely the wrong way around if you are trying to change society to increase GDP. You are increasing GDP to change society.

So, what I would strongly push for is the development of new measures of human welfare. Welfare is much broader than GDP. Two of the greatest inventions of our century have been "retirement" and "the weekend". We have to think of this broader notion of welfare which includes leisure time. It also includes health and life expectancy, particularly healthy life expectancy. Then we should think about using that to evaluate policies. We should be happy to accept policies that lower income, that lower GDP if they increase welfare. An important thing here is to get some measures. We need a measure that is better than GDP.

The other issue is about incentives versus risk pooling. We need incentives to get people to work hard and to do the right thing. We need risk-pooling because a life with high incentives generates enormous risk. These two things are in conflict. The more you pool risks, the less what you do matters for your outcome, the more sharing there is. We should have both. If you go to the circus, you see the trapeze artist flying and jumping from one hoop to another. If you take away the safety net, that trapeze artist will try harder, they will grab on tighter, they will be more frightened and they will work much harder. But they will still sometimes fall. If we have a society that only has incentives but no sharing and no risk pooling, when people fall, it will be disastrous. We should have a safety net, but there is a trade-off.

China recently introduced health insurance and pensions. I think these policies will slow down economic growth in China. One reason for the rapid growth is people are working hard and saving a lot because they are very frightened of being sick in old age. Growth will slow down but we think there will be an enormous increase in welfare from this.

So, if we are going to measure welfare, what should be in it? It should include life expectancy, consumption, health and leisure. I think a real notion of wealth would also include happiness, social networks, children, equality and the environment. The problem is if you want a complete measure, we are never going to get it. It is too difficult. I think we should start with a simple measure that captures some things that are objectively measurable.

GDP is only about market activities, the demand for traded goods and services where we have prices, but it is incredibly misleading if we use it as a policy goal. There are many things that will increase GDP but lower welfare. For example, if we were to make everyone work every weekend in Singapore, GDP would go up but people would not be happy. People like the weekend, they like playing golf, going sailing and spending time with their family. So, I think this move to think about welfare rather than income is an essential one. If you want to measure welfare, we should reduce all these dimensions to one number. We want one aggregate number measuring human welfare.

Data on the "value of life" by income quintile shows that rich people are willing to spend more on life. They will spend more to avoid the risk of death.

"Value" of Life by Income Quintile: United States

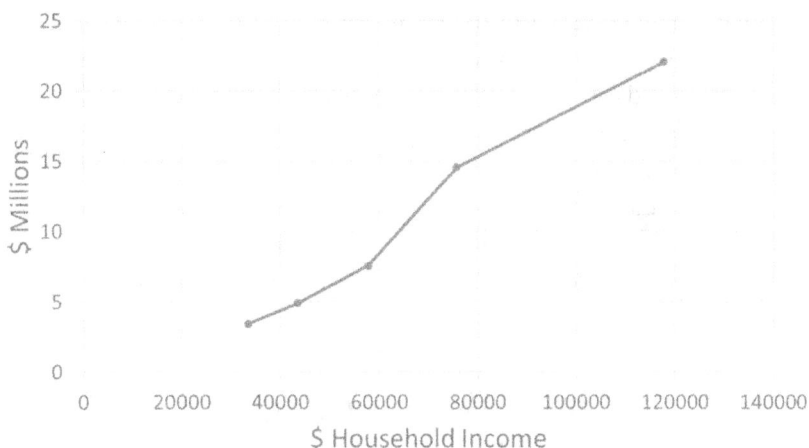

Does this mean that as a society we should value the lives of rich people more? I think that should not be the case. This is really an exchange rate. It is a rate at which people will give up money to buy health. The exchange rate goes two ways. You can work out the exchange rate for the Singapore and the US dollar. It is about 0.7. But you can also go the other way. The rate of exchange for the US dollar for the Singapore dollar is about 1.42. Those are both equally good ways of thinking of an exchange rate. When we do that and we look at the value of money rather than the value of life, we find that the value of money is much higher for poorer people. Poorer people really value money in terms of life-years. To say I would pay a lot for life means I do not value money very much.

What does this mean for you? Up to a million dollars a year, the value of a year lived at a million dollars is about three times that of $27,000. The value of extra money is not actually incredibly high and that is because very rich people are very willing to pay for increases in life. This is another way of saying that they are not willing to pay very much for money.

We calculated income-adjusted life expectancy against GDP per capita for a whole range of countries. The key point is that they are not the same, they are correlated. Rich countries tend to have better life spans and healthier people but they are not the same. Policies that maximise income-adjusted life expectancy and GDP will be quite different.

We also did some analysis using this new measure on the effects of rural pensions and health insurance in China. We think that providing rural health insurance will lower output by about 2.8 per cent. It will lower consumption and capital. The big effect is lowering hours worked. People are working in China to accumulate money to pay for medical bills for themselves or for their families. However, there is a huge increase on welfare with rural health insurance. Its consumption equivalent is about an 11 per cent increase. People really do not like the risk of medical expenses, so you can lower GDP per capita but at the same time increase welfare.

Output and Welfare Effects of Rural Pensions and Health Insurance in China

	Pension Insurance	Health Insurance
Output	-3.10	-2.80
Consumption	-2.65	-3.33
Capital	-4.39	-2.43
Hours worked	-2.00	-9.03
CEV (%)	-2.76	11.35

% change from baseline

China recently relaxed the one-child policy so that families can have two children. We think that this will have a jump-up in fertility to about 1.8 from about 1.5. Some believe that this would be good for population ageing. I think the story is much less clear. If you look at working age shares, it takes about 60 years for the working-age share to move in your favour with higher fertility. That is because it takes 20 years for the children to enter the workforce, but those children also have more children which increase youth dependency rates. So, fertility policies take a very long time to have an impact. In the long run, the higher fertility in China leads to lower income per capita and that is because of a slightly lower female labour market participation and a slightly lower education of children when you have higher fertility.

We know about the enormous income inequality in the US. This is worsened by the fact that the consumption of the highest decile is higher than that of the lowest. They also have higher health utility — their health status is better. They also have much lower mortality — they live longer. The top decile has about seven times the consumption of the lowest decile, but the welfare of the highest decile is about 20 times that of the bottom decile. That is because the highest decile is much healthier and has much lower mortality. This welfare measure brings home this notion that societies can be very unequal. Inequality is much bigger than we think because of this correlation between good health, longevity and income.

Welfare Ratios of Deciles at Age 60

Measure	10/50 ratio	90/50 ratio	90/10 ratio
Welfare	0.23	5.22	23.08
Consumption	0.35	2.65	7.50
Health utility	0.61	1.22	2.00
Flow utility	0.35	3.02	8.71

The enormous advantage in Singapore is that it is not locked into an unsustainable pay-as-you-go system. There is fiscal space for innovation. There is an issue of self-reliance and limited risk pooling. I think there is room for more risk pooling, but this is a judgement question. There will be fewer incentives for risk pooling but Singapore is really at the extreme of not having much risk pooling compared to other countries. In many other countries, I would say they need more incentives and less risk pooling. We talked about rising health and long-term care cost. Here, I think the real issue is value for money. Healthcare is getting more expensive. We are spending more but are we getting value for money? Here, Singapore comes out very well compared to other countries. It has a very cheap healthcare system that produces good health. So, in summary, I think Singapore is already in a very good position. I think by facing up to the fact that the institutions will have to change, this incredible boon of longer healthy lives will become a real asset for Singapore.

CHAPTER 7

Misconceptions that Frame Singaporeans Living Longer as a Liability

KANWALJIT SOIN

In 2016, Singapore was ranked third in the world for the longest average life expectancy and second in the world for the longest average healthy life expectancy. Therefore, we are not only living longer, but we are living longer, healthier. Thus, we cannot equate biological age with chronological age. Seventy is the new 50. Fortunately, as we have grown older, we have also grown richer. Singapore's GDP per capita rose from just S$900 in 1970 to S$71,000 in 2016, one of the highest in the world. Despite the abundance of these good tidings, ageing in Singapore has generally been considered as a liability because of misconceptions about the ageing process and ageism. Policy planners, media, society in general and unfortunately some older people themselves are guilty of harbouring views which associate old age with physical decline, with financial dependence and with degraded mental functions. These misconceptions have clouded the promise of old age.

I will now cite a few misconceptions that some policymakers seem to have internalised and tend to perpetuate. The very important "Population White Paper", conceived by the National Population and Talent Division, to set the direction of our country's future, was presented in Parliament in 2013. Please note this very crucial but non-evidence-based paragraph in this vital document: "For society, a declining old-age support ratio would mean rising taxes and a heavier economic load on a smaller base of working-age

Singaporeans. Companies may not find enough workers". This population planning paper and many policy speeches have highlighted the adverse consequences of a declining old-age support ratio, or if expressed differently, an increasing old age dependency ratio. Both ratios are an incomplete, inaccurate and outmoded view of financial dependence in old age.

The old age support ratio indicates the number of working-age people — people aged 20–64 in the population — who are available to support one older person aged 65 or above. Here, we are assuming that those aged 20 to 64 are engaged productively and those who are over 65 would have to be suddenly supported from their 65th birthday onwards by their younger stalwarts. In reality, many Singaporeans over 65 are economically active and contribute either directly or indirectly to economic and social robustness. Also, if a retiree has saved enough money for his or her remaining life, should he or she be counted as dependent economically? We need alternative measures to reflect the true economic dependency of the elderly.

One such measure is a savings-adjusted old-age support ratio that requires an adjustment for savings available to the elderly. Or if you define those who must be supported as aged over 70 and not over 65, the old-age support ratio becomes much more favourable. With lower birth rates, total dependency ratio has gone down, but we hardly ever hear this fact being articulated. We only hear of old-age dependency ratio; however, it is but one part of the total dependency ratio. The same cut-off age of 65 is used to operationalise old-age dependency ratio even for 2030. There is no recognition of the cohort effects of better health and longer working lives of people in 2030. It is often assumed that the experience of the present can be extrapolated into the future. The 65-year olds of 2030 will be healthier, less dependent and more mentally agile than ever before, and so economic projections must take that into account.

Another alarmist view that is often articulated by policymakers is that, with an ageing population, business activity would slow and job and employment opportunities would shrink. In contrast to this pessimism about business affairs, global professional services firm Deloitte says "ageing populations will generate a growth cluster of new business opportunities for this region and Singapore in particular." The silver economy will see growth in private healthcare, travel, pharmaceuticals, biotechnology, insurance and retail industries. With relatively high levels of asset ownership among older

Singaporeans, there is an increased demand for the management of these assets, and this is generating opportunities in the financial services sector, insurance and legal industry. The Deloitte report further ranked Singapore third out of 15 Asia Pacific countries for silver market potential. With Singaporeans continuing to work and earning an income for a longer period, seniors are increasingly becoming consumers and paying at least Goods and Services Tax (GST).

Hence, older people are not just dependents, which is the only role in which they are cast. Policymakers often point to the intergenerational conflict arising from the financial dependency of ageing populations, but unlike other countries and thanks to the foresight of earlier policymakers, the reality here is quite different. The CPF system encourages self-reliance by making each individual responsible for his or her own retirement needs, rather than burdening future generations with ever increasing taxes and thus minimising potential intergenerational stresses as outlined by Professor Canning. We must also consider private intra-familial transfers, from older to younger generations — how many of us have helped our children to buy their first apartment or first car?

Ageism, in my opinion, is a mammoth misconception about the ageing process. Ageism is defined as a negative stereotyping of, and discrimination against, individuals or a group of individuals because of their age. Misperceptions regarding the ability, motivation and cognitive states of older persons abound among society and policymakers. Where cognition is concerned, research shows that psychological functions do not decline gradually in the healthy, elderly person. Instead, they plateau until a late age. This is due to improvement in crystallised intelligence as we grow older. This type of intelligence refers to the use of accumulated knowledge and experience in decision-making at older ages.

Now, I will point to some links between age discrimination and policies in Singapore and how they tend to convert Singaporeans from assets to liabilities. We are all aware that Singapore is not a welfare state. Social spending in Singapore only amounts to 5.5 per cent of GDP. In China, it is 8 per cent and it is an average of 21 per cent in other OECD countries. The social safety net in Singapore is built on the key principles of self-reliance and family as the two most important lines of support. Policymakers and the government have drilled this concept of self-reliance into our psyche and many older people want to continue to work. The presence of ageism and age discrimination, however, has trapped older Singaporeans between a rock and a hard place, where employment is concerned. The retirement age in Singapore is only 62. In the first place, why do we need a retirement age when there is no formal pension system? There is a heterogeneity where ageing is concerned. People do not age at the same rate and should not be retiring at the same age. Australia and the US have no mandatory retirement age as that has been abolished.

From 1 July 2017, employers must offer re-employment to eligible employees who turn 62 up to the age of 67. However, even if the employee is lucky enough to be re-employed and continues with the same job, the wages are often reduced and the contract is renewable annually. Also, termination of service can be done at any time without any reason by serving notice as stipulated in the contract. If the employer thinks that the employee cannot be offered re-employment, then the company can offer a one-off employment assistance of three and a half months of salary, and that is the end of the matter. The Ministry of Manpower has acknowledged that specific anti-discrimination laws may be needed to deal with age discrimination in employment here. However, companies argue that too much government protection is bad for business but the Ministry of Manpower has countered with the argument that the global competitiveness of places with anti-discrimination laws has remained relatively stable. Countries like the US, Britain, Germany, Hong Kong and Japan have been cited. Yet, the government is not willing to pass legislation to make re-employment compulsory till 67.

On the other side of the coin, older people are still expected to be self-reliant. In fact, because of age discrimination, many perfectly healthy, older workers feel that they have been forced by circumstances into leaving the labour force. Yet, we bemoan the lack of workers for our economy. In addition, being denied a job will impact on the CPF savings of these individuals and this may lead to financial dependency on the family and community. That age discrimination exists in employment has been acknowledged by our policymakers and by research published by the Institute of Policy Studies (IPS). In 2014 Mdm Halimah Yacob, then the Speaker of Parliament and now our President had this to say: "We are still very much an ageist society. Sometimes, people may not even know they are being ageist. I receive a lot of feedback from elderly job applicants and they say it is very difficult for them to get a job."

When Deputy Prime Minister Tharman Shanmugaratnam was speaking at the budget forum in 2015, he acknowledged that ageism in Singapore workplaces meant that experienced older workers were being shut out of jobs. He said: "I think we have to tackle ageism in Singapore. There is a sort of a quiet, unstated discrimination among the mid-careers and those who are in their 50s." IPS' latest survey in 2017 shows that there is an overwhelming agreement on age discrimination for workers aged 55 years and above, who are looking for work. Despite this big hurdle of age discrimination, older people still want to be self-reliant and the employment rate for local residents, aged 55 to 64, increased to 67 per cent in 2016, one of the highest compared to other OECD countries. For those between 65 and 69, it was 43 per cent; and for those over 70, it was 15 per cent.

The median age of our workforce is 43 years across all sectors and we can anticipate it to reach 47 years by 2020. Currently, one in three workers is already 50 years old and over. Soon, they will constitute most of our workforce. This is our reality — there is no place for age discrimination. How well we adapt our employment culture and how well we eliminate ageism from our employment practices will determine Singapore's future economic and social viability.

Media also plays an important role in the negative framing of the elderly. In television shows, for example, aunties and uncles are all too often portrayed as bumbling old fools. Our society of older people is frequently referred to in the media as a "silver tsunami" or a "demographic time bomb" as if it was a destructive force. The ways in which the elderly are represented in the media can have a lasting impact on social attitudes and this reinforces negative stereotypes held by both younger and older people. Sadly, this becomes a self-fulfilling prophecy for older people and can impact on older people's confidence and quality of life. The biggest problem for many older people is ageism rather than the process of ageing itself.

Let me now cite an example of when ignorance about ageism is not bliss. In 2016, the government unveiled its S$3 billion action plan for successful ageing. This is an impressive plan and provides a framework for preparing for our transition to becoming a super-aged society in 2030. Without a good hard look at the effects of ageism on the ability of individuals to age successfully, we may not manage the transition well. We need plans, policies and action, not just for active ageing, but also for understanding the causes of ageism and reducing all forms of age discrimination. The 2015 World Health Organization's *World Report on Ageing and Health* made this important observation and I quote: "Age-based stereotypes influence behaviours, policy development and even research. Addressing these by combating ageism must lie at the core of any public health response to population ageing." Alas, there is no mention of any action against ageism in Singapore's action plan for successful ageing.

While ageing is a dynamic process and is changing all the time, there is a structural lag of many years between the practice of public policy and the lived experiences of older people. Because of the stereotyping of older people as part of the past, we are often overlooked in society's future. In contrast, if older Singaporeans were considered as an asset, there will be a different orientation towards health and social expenditure for this group of citizens.

IV

Dialogue

8

Dialogue with Finance Minister Heng Swee Keat: Strategic Planning for Singapore's Future

HENG SWEE KEAT

The budget is a strategic plan for Singapore. The budget cannot just be about taxes, revenue and expenditure. Why are we collecting revenue? What for and where are we spending it? Why are we spending it? Are we planning for the long haul? Are we planning for a better Singapore? I think those are the important questions. These are the issue that I think we ought to concentrate on. It is not just what the budget can do or what government can do but what all of us in Singapore can do together.

Let me start with a preview of the budget. First, government spending has more than doubled in the last decade from S$33 billion in the financial year 2007 to S$71 billion in the financial year 2016. This is a very high rate of increase. So, the question is where has the money gone to? If you just concentrate on social spending, it has gone up from 35 per cent of S$33 billion in 2007 to 40 per cent of S$71 billion in 2017.

The Ministry of Education (MOE) accounted for 22.8 per cent of the pie in 2007. In 2016, it was 17.7 per cent. So, are we spending less on education? No, because the whole pie has grown. We are spending more on education despite the fact that we are having falling enrolments and we are closing schools. Yet, we are spending more. We are spending more per child and per individual. This is partly because we are spending more in our schools and in the Institutes of Higher Learning (IHLs) and because we have extended programmes like SkillsFuture and other lifelong learning programmes. That is the part of our social budget.

The Ministry of Health (MOH) accounted for 6.7 per cent of S$33 billion, and last year, it more than doubled to 13.7 per cent of a much, much bigger base of S$71 billion. The Ministry of Social and Family Development (MSF) expenditures accounted for 3.5 per cent of the total expenditure. The Ministry of Culture, Community and Youth (MCCY) accounted for 3 per cent and a segment of manpower expenditures dealing with workers like worker upgrading has gone up as well. So, our social spending has gone up significantly.

While the overall percentage of security spending has come down, the absolute number has continued to go up. In terms of infrastructure and transport, the one very interesting set of numbers is from the Ministry of Transport (MOT). MOT accounted for 5.9 per cent of the budget in 2007 and it has gone up to 14.6 per cent in 2016. So, again it has more than doubled. Why? It is not only the spending on infrastructure like rail lines and maintenance work, but also the new bus services, the bus services plan and very significant changes within just ten years.

Now, where did the money come from? The one data point which I hope that everyone here can bear in mind is that back in 2007, the contribution from the reserves was 5.6 per cent and in 2016, the contribution from the reserves was 17.3 per cent. Of all revenue sources, it is the single largest contribution category today — more than corporate income tax, GST or personal income tax. To put it another way, if we had not used contributions from reserves, your personal income tax, GST or corporate income tax could have doubled. All of these are not terribly great solutions. So, I know that many of you, as shown in the survey, think that we should be spending more reserves and it is a subject which we can discuss in detail. For now, I thought that we must have some perspective on where the money is coming from.

Let me move on to three new topics. I will talk about three issues to set the stage for further discussion. Firstly, we are undergoing a major demographic transition. This major demographic transition would have implications on many of the issues that you and I and every Singaporean, everyone living in Singapore, is concerned with. Whether it is an issue relating to healthcare, financial adequacy, mobility, transport, jobs or the future economy, each and every one of these issues is a very big topic by itself. I think we ought to drill deep into each of these issues to understand what it all means.

For instance, in healthcare, how would the demand pattern change in the coming years as our population goes through that demographic transition? What sort of illness will be more prevalent and how would that manifest itself? On the supply side, do we have enough doctors, healthcare workers and healthcare professionals to manage the transition? Do we have enough of the right expertise? Where is the care best done? Is it in the acute hospital or in the community hospital? Is it in a community? Is it at home? For each of these, what are the pros and cons? How do we go about deciding on what is the best system? It is not just looking at it from the point of view of an acute hospital versus a community hospital. We should look at it as totality and ask what the best way of dealing with it is. What is the best way of managing it so that we can be successful? The same applies to education, defence and security. Our changing demographic pattern will have a significant impact on each of these single item issues. For example, what does changing demography mean for the economy? It is going to be a significant set of changes. My first point is that each issue requires very useful and deep discussion.

Secondly, beyond a single issue, we really must think of these issues together. How would issue A interact with issue B? How would healthcare interact with the economy, jobs and social care? If we were to take a segmented approach and say this is issue A, this is issue B and this is issue C, and we tackle each one separately, I think we are going to be lost. This is because we might be working across purpose and the outcome may not be as good as if we work together. When I was in MOE, and even now in MOF, I saw the large number of cross-disciplinary, interdisciplinary study centres, policy think tanks and so on, across all universities in the world. This is a new growth industry. If studying an issue requires so much work and cross-disciplinary effort, how much more do we need to do if we are going to do something about an issue? The policy work and the actual work related to an issue will be far better dealt with by a cross-disciplinary approach. Therefore, for many of these issues, we need to take that view.

Let me just give you two illustrations of what I mean. One is the interaction between work, health and financial security. I think many of you are aware that Japan is also facing a very rapidly ageing population. In Japan, they found that the older workers who continued working, regardless of whether they needed the income or not, were healthier. This is because work provides a platform for social interaction which staying at home just does not provide. So, we cannot be thinking about work in isolation from health and financial security.

The second example has got to do with our own experience with health and social care. When we first started the Pioneer Generation Package (PGP), we were quite concerned as to whether our pioneer generation would understand the intricacies of the scheme. We then appointed pioneer generation ambassadors — neighbours staying in the vicinity — who would go out and explain this package to our pioneer generation. Interestingly, there were many who raised issues which were not about healthcare. There were issues relating to finance, their family members, staying alone and loneliness and needing other sources of care. For every one of those issues, there is an agency, ministry or people responsible, but there is clearly a gap at the frontline. There is a gap in terms of how well we are delivering that service to the seniors who need it. So, we piloted the idea of "pioneer generation ambassadors" and achieved some good outcomes.

At the last budget, I had a very good discussion with Minister Gan Kim Yong and we decided that we will look at a community network of seniors. The community network of seniors also comprised neighbours staying in the vicinity and neighbourhood who would explain to the seniors in their area about some of the activities around them and asked them what their needs were. They have come up with very interesting results. We were able to meet a very important and growing need in our society. We need to look at the issues in a much more cross-disciplinary way and across agencies and ministries. Just some weeks back, I had a very interesting discussion with Minister Gan Kim Yong, Minister Grace Fu, Minister Desmond Lee and Speaker Tan Chuan-Jin because all of them are very concerned about the issues of seniors. We had an excellent discussion on what we need to do differently in the coming years.

A few days back, I read in *The Straits Times* and in the *New York Times International Edition* that the UK has appointed a Minister of Loneliness. Now, I must say that the UK must be the first country in the world to appoint a Minister of Loneliness. A report from the Joe Cox Commission found that nine million people are either often or are always feeling lonely. The sense of loneliness actually affects all age groups but it affects the elderly even more. Majority of those who are 75 and above live alone. I notice that as well in my own work in the constituency. Now, interestingly, after the report came out, the UK was the first to act.

It is not alone. The former Surgeon General of the US then estimated that in the US, 40 per cent suffer from loneliness of some form. Being a former Surgeon General, he talked about how that is a health epidemic. So, it is very important for us not to look at issues in isolation. I am really very glad that my colleagues in the Ministries are dealing with this. Ministers Kim Yong, Grace, Desmond and Speaker Chuan-Jin have been very concerned and have been working together on this. We started this work a lot earlier, and in fact, Minister Gan Kim Yong and Minister Desmond Lee co-chaired a Committee on Ageing. They have been doing a lot of work. So, we are actually not starting from scratch, we are starting from a position of strength and I hope that we can do more. I will be happy to hear your views on what we can do on this front.

My third point concerns the implications of this change on Singapore and ageing as a global phenomenon. We are not the only society that is ageing rapidly, many other societies are and what are the implications? There are pluses and minuses. The plus is that we can now work with many more countries to see how we can tackle common challenges, in particular in the area of healthcare. Solutions that are tried in one place could probably be useful to Singapore and so on. Hopefully, the global budget for doing research in this area will increase and we can all do it together.

The minus is this: we do not know how ageing will affect other societies. In fact, we cannot even be sure how ageing will affect our own society. What is the impact on the psychology of our people? Do our people become more withdrawn as we have seen in some societies? Will there be a withdrawal from the global system? Globalisation is not something to be taken for granted because if the stresses and strains are great, partly because of ageing and the inability of older workers to train, retrain and learn new things, you can expect that many other societies would think about protecting themselves first. They will first make their own society great again before thinking about the impact on others. What is the impact on us in that scenario? Now, fortunately, I must say that it is to the great credit of former Minister George Yeo, who started the wave of Free Trade Agreement almost 20 years ago, that we now have a whole range of free trade agreements. It provides a bit of insulation, but is not something to be taken for granted. The global order can change very quickly. I do not think anybody would have expected that America would withdraw from the Trans-Pacific Partnership (TPP) just like that, but it happened. Let us be very careful about what is happening globally.

Of the other two global forces that are going to have a significant impact on us, the first is advances in technology. The Germans talk about Industry 4.0, and there is a very lively debate on this whole issue of how information and communication technology (ICT) will affect even the traditional manufacturing industry. The impact of ICT and of technology in general on many industries will not be easy to predict. What is the impact of genomics on healthcare? What is the impact of genomics and ICT, together, on healthcare? A whole new range of issues have been thrown up, not just the social and ethical issue, but also very important economic issues. While we talk about our ageing population and how we need to prepare our older workers better for changes, we have to bear in mind that our education system was not as good as it is today when we first became independent. In fact, many of my classmates in my primary school did not make it past the Primary School Leaving Examinations (PSLE) and they started work when they were very young. Retraining some of these older workers today is going to be quite difficult.

So, fortunately, I think our education system has improved a great deal but when we talk about the future of work, industry and technology, we have to take a concerted effort to think about how we can redesign jobs. We may need to think about how to extend the retirement age, and for that matter, rethink the whole concept of retirement. Why should people retire? Even as we do that, we should be very careful that we do not deprive the young people of opportunities. What is the balance we need to create in our society to manage that? It is not a simple issue but an issue which we ought to grapple with early. The technological changes throughout the global economy will affect each and every one of us regardless of our age and it will affect our elder workers even more.

I just saw some of the initiatives that have been tried out in Japan. There, they are looking at the use of robots to enable older workers to continue to do fairly difficult manual jobs because the robot takes over the hard work of lifting heavy boxes which enables the elder person to continue working. I went to factories in Singapore recently and looked at how they redesigned jobs to enable this lady, who is now in her late 50s, to continue working in that company. I was really very impressed. So, I asked the management. I said, "Did you do this deliberately or did it happen as an afterthought?" They said, "No, we are very conscious that we must use technology because otherwise we will be displaced as a company. At the same time we also want to create opportunities for the workers who have been with us for so many years so loyally, and therefore, we make a special effort to redesign jobs." I said, "Well, you are a very global company. What are you doing elsewhere?" They are indeed doing something similar elsewhere. My respect for this company went up a few notches. I was really happy that we have such a company in Singapore. So, that is about the future of how you will interact with technology.

Now, the other final global force that I want to talk about is the shifting economic fortunes. This graph, from McKinsey Global Institute, shows an approximation of centres of gravity of the global economy from AD1 to today. Essentially, in the earlier part, Asia was the centre of many economic activities for many years. China and India were agricultural economies and had mastered agriculture. They were the most successful countries in growing their population and their economy. But gradually, it shifted to England as it was England which started the Industrial Revolution. The Industrial Revolution spread to the rest of Europe and then, thereafter, moved over to America. And the centre of gravity of the global economy moved westwards to the US. Then gradually, as the Asian economies re-joined the global economy, given their weight, the centre of gravity started shifting back. And there are some projections that over the next five years or ten years, the centre of gravity will continue moving to this part of the world.

Now, this is going to happen at a time when many economies in Asia are also ageing. What would be the impact of an ageing economy as well as a growing and technologically more advanced global economy for all of us here? I do not think I have the full answer. I have seen many reports speculating on the future of jobs, industry and fortunes. I am not prepared to bet that it will be one way or the other, but I am prepared to bet that it will be different. The more alert we are to this, the better it is.

To sum up, I would say that when we think about the ageing issue, it is important that we do not look at it as a single issue. Neither should we look at it from an agency-centric point of view. It is important for us within Singapore to work across, not just within government agencies, but with the people and private sector. What is it that a private sector should do differently — in the way they think about the economy, jobs and their role in providing some of the support? What is the role of our Voluntary Welfare Organisations (VWO)? What is it that we can do in our own neighbourhoods? What is it that you and I can do together?

What we are seeing is not a single change but really a series of changes happening across space and time. How are these changes going to interact with one another? We cannot predict with accuracy, so what is the best way of dealing with it? I think we can be sure that the rate of change will be faster not just for us but for everyone else around the world. It means that it can be more unsettling and it is all the more critical that we stay together to tackle these changes. If we can put our minds and hearts together, I think we can do a lot more. So, yes, the population is ageing but we can be an ageless society.

About the Contributors

David CANNING is Richard Saltonstall Professor of Population Sciences and Professor of Economics and International Health at the Department of Global Health and Population, Harvard T.H. Chan School of Public Health. He has a PhD in economics from Cambridge University, and has held faculty positions at the London School of Economics, Cambridge University, Columbia University, and Queen's University Belfast.

He has carried out extensive research on the impact of health improvements on economic outcomes and served as a member of Working Group One of the World Health Organization's Commission on Macroeconomics and Health. Along with David Bloom he originated the concept of the Demographic Dividend, looking at how changes in fertility and age structure affect macroeconomic performance. His current work focuses on economic and social policy responses to population ageing.

CHAN Heng Chee is Ambassador-at-Large with the Singapore Foreign Ministry. She chairs the Lee Kuan Yew Centre for Innovative Cities in the Singapore University of Technology and Design. She is Chairman of the National Arts Council, a member of the Presidential Council for Minority Rights, the 2016 Constitutional Commission, and the Presidential Elections Commission. She is also Deputy Chairman of the Social Science Research Council.

Ambassador Chan is a member of the National University of Singapore Board of Trustees, and a member of the Yale-NUS Governing Board. She also serves as member of the Executive Board of the China Cultural Centre, and the Advisory Council of Temasek Foundation Connects. She was elected the Global Co-Chair of the Asia Society in December 2017, and a Council Member of the Asia Society Policy Institute.

Previously, she was Singapore's Ambassador to the United States, and Singapore's Permanent Representative to the United Nations with concurrent accreditation as High Commissioner to Canada and Ambassador to Mexico.

Janadas DEVAN, Director of the Institute of Policy Studies, was educated at the National University of Singapore and Cornell University in the United States. He taught English in various institutions in Singapore and the US, and later wrote for various publications in the region, before joining The Straits Times in 1997.

He served as the paper's leader writer for many years, writing unsigned editorials on a wide variety of subjects. He wrote a weekly column on politics and economics, in which he covered international and domestic developments, and a column on language for The Sunday Times. He became the editor of the paper's opinion pages in 2008, and the paper's Associate Editor in 2010. He also did a weekly radio broadcast, "Call from America", for Radio Singapore International, from 2000 to 2008, on American life and society.

He left The Straits Times in July 2012 on being appointed the Government's Chief of Communications at the Ministry of Communications and Information. He is now concurrently Deputy Secretary at the Prime Minister's Office.

Christopher GEE is Senior Research Fellow at the Institute of Policy Studies, where he leads the Governance and Economy Department. He has published several papers on retirement financing, strengthening old-age income support, and managing healthcare costs for an ageing population. He was previously in investment banking, leading equity research teams covering Singapore and Malaysia, and the Asian real estate sector. He has a BA (Law) from the University of Nottingham and holds the CFA charter.

He holds a joint appointment with the National University of Singapore's Department of Real Estate and the Institute of Real Estate Studies, and is a non-executive director of CapitaLand Retail China Trust, a Singapore-listed real estate investment trust with a portfolio of shopping malls in China.

HENG Swee Keat is the Minister for Finance and Member of Parliament for Tampines Group Representation Constituency (GRC). The Ministry of Finance manages the national budget, oversees corporate governance regulations, and supervises the prudent investment and utilisation of public funds and government reserves. Mr Heng co-chaired the Committee on the Future Economy (CFE), which charted the strategies for Singapore's next phase of growth. He chairs the tripartite Future Economy Council, which oversees the implementation of national strategies in areas such as skills and capabilities development, innovation and productivity, and industry transformation. He is also the Deputy Chairman of the National Research Foundation, which sets the direction for Singapore's research, innovation and enterprise strategies.

Before this, Mr Heng served as Minister for Education from 2011 to 2015. He drove programmes for a student-centric, values-driven education system, emphasising the holistic development of students and multiple educational pathways. While at MOE, Mr Heng also led Our Singapore Conversation, a national consultation exercise that reached out to close to 50,000 Singaporeans on their aspirations for Singapore's future. In 2015, he chaired the Singapore 50 (SG50) Steering Committee leading the celebrations for Singapore's Golden Jubilee.

Prior to entering politics in May 2011, Mr Heng was the Managing Director of the Monetary Authority of Singapore (MAS), where he received the "Central Bank Governor of the Year in Asia-Pacific" Award by the British magazine The Banker. He has served in various other public service positions, including appointments in the Singapore Police Force, as the Permanent Secretary of the Ministry of Trade and Industry, as the Chief Executive Officer of the Trade Development Board, and as the Principal Private Secretary to then-Senior Minister Lee Kuan Yew from 1997 to 2000. In 2001, Mr Heng was awarded the Gold Medal in Public Administration, and the Meritorious Medal in 2010 for his contribution to the public service in Singapore.

Mr Heng has an MA in Economics from Cambridge University. He also holds a Masters in Public Administration from the Kennedy School of Government, Harvard University.

Laurence LIEN is Co-Founder and Chief Executive Officer of the Asia Philanthropy Circle, a membership-based platform for Asian philanthropists to exchange, learn and collaborate. He is also Chairman of Lien Foundation, a family foundation that takes a radical approach in the fields of education, eldercare and the environment. He was the Chief Executive Officer of the National Volunteer & Philanthropy Centre from 2008 to 2014, when he launched the Community Foundation of Singapore and is currently its Chairman.

Prior to serving in the non-profit sector, he was a civil servant. Mr Lien holds degrees from Oxford University, the National University of Singapore, and Harvard University's Kennedy School of Government. He was also a Nominated Member of Parliament in Singapore from 2012 to 2014.

Ravi MENON has been Managing Director of the Monetary Authority of Singapore (MAS) since 2011. On the international front, he is a member of the Financial Stability Board (FSB) Steering Committee. He chaired the FSB Standing Committee on Standards Implementation from 2013 to 2017, the International Monetary and Financial Committee (IMFC) Deputies Meetings from 2011 to 2015, and the APEC Senior Officials Meetings in 2009. He was Permanent Secretary of the Ministry of Trade and Industry (2007 to 2011) and Deputy Secretary at the Ministry of Finance (2003 to 2007), where he was responsible for fiscal policy and government reserves.

Mr Menon began his career at MAS in 1987. During his 16 years in MAS, he was involved in monetary policy, econometric forecasting, banking regulation and liberalisation, and integrated supervision of complex financial institutions. A recipient of the Public Administration Medal (Gold), he has served on boards in the public, private, and people sectors. Mr Menon is currently Chairman of the Institute of Banking and Finance, and he serves on the Board of Trustees of the Singapore Indian Development Association, a community volunteer group.

He holds a Masters in Public Administration from Harvard University, and a Bachelor of Social Science (Honours) in Economics from the National University of Singapore.

Kanwaljit SOIN is a practising medical specialist, and Singapore's first female Nominated Member of Parliament from 1992 to 1996. She is a founder of many civil society organisations including WINGS (Women's Initiative for Ageing Successfully) and AWARE (Association of Women for Action and Research). She was a global ambassador of UK-based HelpAge International, which serves disadvantaged older people worldwide. She has served as a board member of Washington University International Advisory Council for Asia. She has also been a jury member for the Rolex Awards for Enterprise.

In 2000, she was presented the "Women Who Make a Difference" Award by the International Women's Forum, Washington DC. In 2006, Dr Soin was presented with the Lifetime Achievement Award by the United Nations Development Fund for Women (Unifem) Singapore for her selfless contribution to society, especially towards the less advantaged. She was named Singapore's "Her World Woman of the Year" in 1992, and was inducted to the Singapore Women's Hall of Fame in 2014.

Sean TAN leads Mercer's career and talent consulting services in Singapore. He has 15 years of consulting and corporate human resource (HR) practitioner experience. His recent consulting engagements were on industry-wide job redesign, competency framework development and workforce study initiatives. His other recent work includes HR strategy and effectiveness (including HR operating model review, talent management practices and career architectures), performance management, workforce analytics, competency modelling as well as compensation structure design.

Prior to Mercer, Mr Tan was Vice President of HR in a leading global investment firm. He also managed the talent graduate programme and held a HR business partnering role to a key business unit. Before that, he held various senior positions in the information communications and technology (ICT) and public sectors, including the Head of Talent Development and Succession Planning, Head of Workforce Planning and Analytics and Head of Talent Acquisition.

TEO Chee Hean was appointed Deputy Prime Minister in 2009. He also serves, since 2011, as Coordinating Minister for National Security. He is Minister in charge of the Civil Service, oversees the Prime Minister's Office Strategy Group, including the National Population and Talent Division and the National Climate Change Secretariat, and is Chairman of the National Research Foundation.

He was awarded the President's Scholarship and the Singapore Armed Forces (SAF) Scholarship in 1973. He graduated with a Bachelor of Science (First Class Honours) in Electrical Engineering and Management Science from the University of Manchester in 1976. He subsequently attained a Masters of Science degree (with distinction) in Computing Science in 1977 at the Imperial College in London, and a Masters in Public Administration at the Kennedy School of Government in Harvard University in 1986, where he was named a Littauer Fellow.

In December 1992, he left the SAF to seek elected public office and was elected as a Member of Parliament in a by-election in the Marine Parade Group Representation Constituency (GRC). He was re-elected to Parliament five times in the Pasir Ris-Punggol GRC.

He has served as Minister for Home Affairs, Minister for Defence, Minister for Education, and Minister for the Environment. He has also served as Minister of State in the Ministries of Finance, Communications and Defence.

ANNEX

Harnessing Singapore's Longevity Dividends: The Generational Economy, Society and Polity

CHRISTOPHER GEE, YVONNE ARIVALAGAN
& CHAO FENGQING

AN INTRODUCTION TO DEMOGRAPHIC OR LONGEVITY DIVIDENDS

Population matters have always been an integral part of Singapore's national development story, given that we are a small city-state with no natural resources. The post-Second World War baby boom, coupled with substantial human capital investments in health and education and followed by fertility decline, allowed Singapore to capture its first demographic dividend.

This first demographic dividend arose from the greater proportion of people of working ages engaged in productive employment relative to those who consume more than they earn (predominantly the young and the old). This contributed to about a third of Singapore's GDP per capita growth in the period between 1965 and 2000 (Bloom & Williamson, 1998, Ogawa et al., 2009).

The drop in fertility that contributed to the first demographic dividend, however, also leads to its reversal as the population ages (see Fig. 1, page 97), with growth in old-age population exceeding growth in the labour force, leading to lower economic growth assuming no change in output per worker, labour force participation and employment rates[1]. The Institute of Policy

---

[1] Singapore reached an inflection point in 2012 when, after over 30 years of an improving trend, the country's age-dependency ratio began to rise as the increase in

95

SINGAPORE PERSPECTIVES 2018

Studies (IPS) projects that Singapore's old-age dependency ratio will rise by more than ten-fold, from having just under nine elder Singaporeans for every 100 persons of working age in 1980, to 91 elder Singaporeans per 100 working age persons in 2080. We estimate this reversal of the first demographic dividend from population ageing to represent a drag of 1.5% points on Singapore's annual GDP per capita growth from 2011 to 2060 (Fig. 2, page 98).

---

old-age dependency ratio overtakes that of the young-age dependency ratio. The age-dependency ratio takes the ages between 20 and 64 as the years that approximate best to the working ages. The young-age dependency is the ratio of population aged 19 and below to 100 persons aged between 20 and 64, whilst the old-age dependency is the ratio of population aged 65 years and above to 100 persons aged between 20 and 64. The total age-dependency ratio is the sum of the young-age and old-age dependency ratios.

Fig. 1. Singapore Population Pyramids: Age Structure of the Population (1980–2080)

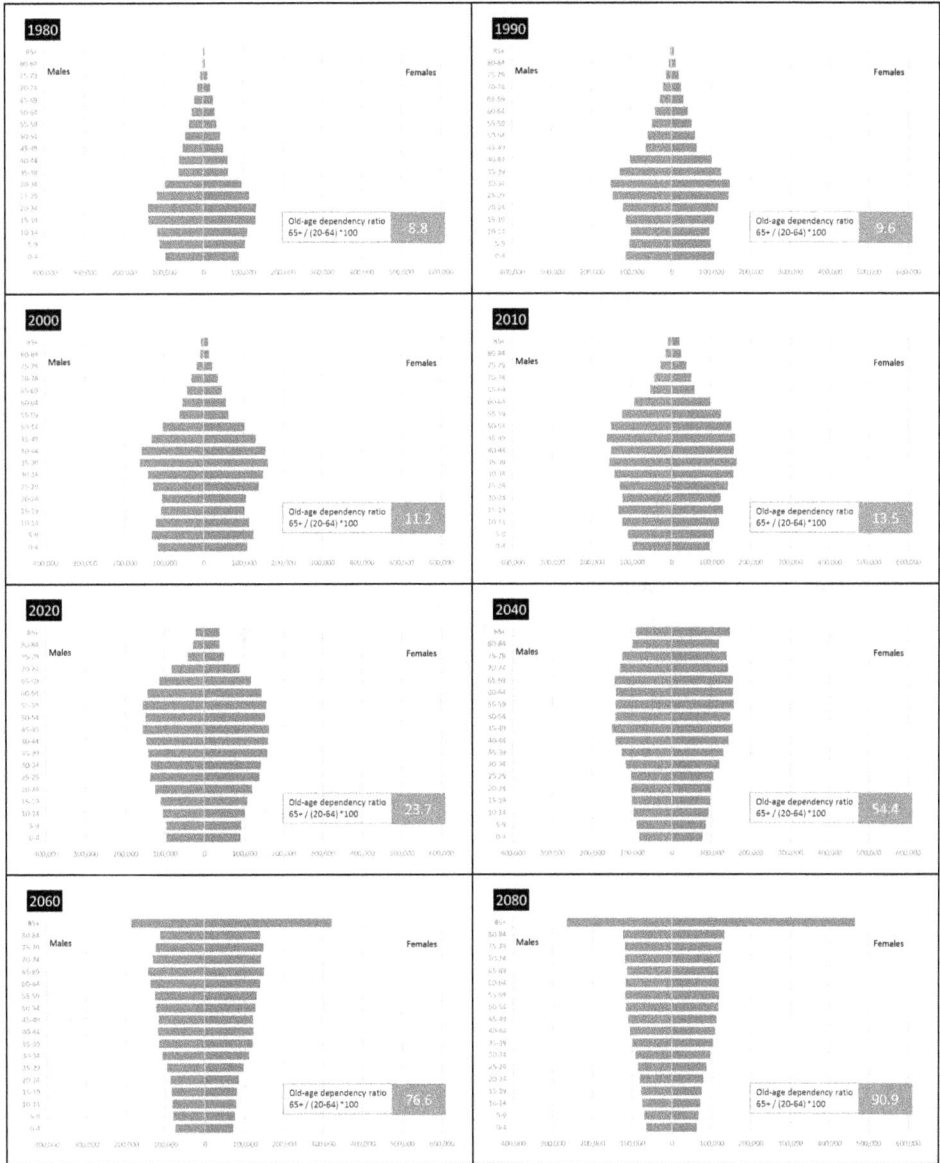

Source: Department of Statistics, Census of Population for 1980–2010; Institute of Policy Studies projections for 2020 onwards. See footnote 1 for the definition of the old-age dependency ratio.

Fig. 2. Singapore's Economic Support Ratio[2] (1960–2100)

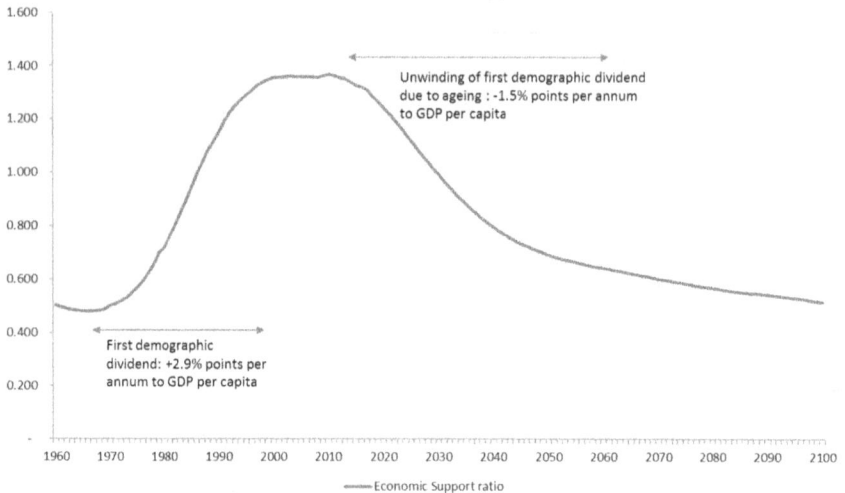

Source: Institute of Policy Studies estimates[3]

The loss of economic productive potential from the changing age structure of the population may be mitigated through immigration (which we consider in a later part of this background paper, see page 107), or may be offset with other demographic or longevity dividends.

---

[2] The Economic Support Ratio is the ratio of effective producers to effective consumers. This metric modifies the traditional support ratio calculation that counts each person of working age (say, 20–64 years) as supporting dependents (0–19, 65+ years) equally. In reality, effective economic productivity and consumption varies considerably by age, and the Economic Support Ratio weighs producers and consumers according to their age-specific profiles of labour income and consumption.

[3] IPS' resident population projections from 2017–2100 are based on an assumed total fertility rate of 1.3 births per woman, increase in life expectancy at birth of 2.0 years in each decade, and net in-migration of 20,000 per annum.

OTHER LONGEVITY DIVIDENDS: HEALTH, EDUCATION, SAVINGS/INVESTMENTS AND TECHNOLOGY

The conditions that eventually result in an ending of the first demographic dividend may, however, lead to a second dividend (Mason and Lee, 2006), assuming individuals and the government are forward-looking and respond to the effects of an ageing workforce and population. With longer life expectancy, individuals have greater incentives to invest in their human capital, especially in health and education. Such increased investments in human capital should result in improved productivity over potentially longer working lifespans.

Another societal response to living longer can also be the accumulation of savings to help sustain consumption at older ages. If invested effectively in the domestic economy, these savings can result in capital deepening and an increase in productivity per worker. If invested abroad, those savings would lead to an increase in gross national income.

We highlight these sources of demographic (or what we might call longevity) dividends below.

HEALTHSPAN

At around 83 years as of 2017, Singapore's life expectancy is among the highest in the world. Singapore's health-adjusted life expectancy (HALE), which estimates the average number of years a person can live in full health, has also been rising. Between 2005 and 2015, male and female life expectancy at birth rose from 77.6 and 82.5 years to 80.5 and 85.1 years, respectively, an increase of 2.9 years for males and 2.5 years for females. HALE for both sexes increased about 1.7 years over that period (Fig. 3, next page).

If these gains in HALE are projected into the future, there will be almost 860,000 healthy Singaporeans 65 years and above in 2030, more than double the number in 2015. Elder Singaporeans aged 65 years and above will have an additional 450,000 healthy life years in 2030 as compared to that cohort in 2015; this represents human capital potential of more than one-fifth the size of the resident labour force in 2015. The likelihood is that the 2030 cohort of elder Singaporeans will also be better educated than their predecessors, extending the productivity potential even further (see next section).

Fig. 3. Singapore Resident Male and Female Health-Adjusted Life Expectancy (HALE)

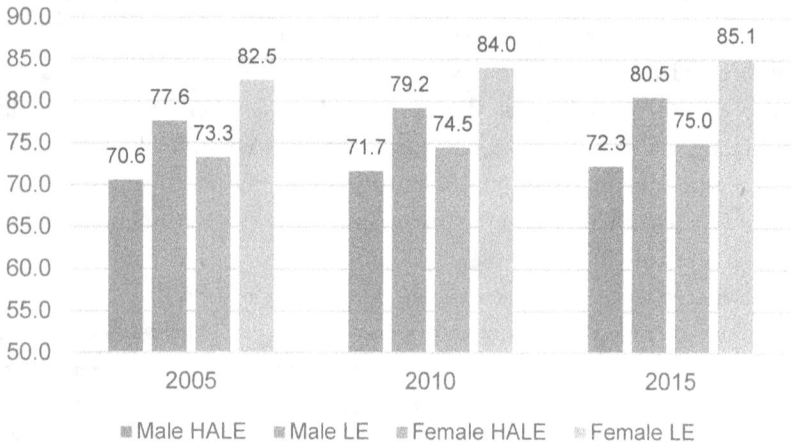

Source: Ministry of Health, 2017, Population and Vital Statistics

Note, however, that whilst HALE for Singaporean residents increased in the 10-year period to 2015, overall life expectancy at birth increased even more, indicating that, despite enjoying more healthy years, Singaporeans are living more years in an unhealthy state, mainly with chronic long-term diseases, including mental health issues, disability and mobility limitations.

To ensure this longevity dividend is captured, the health policy objective becomes not only that of extending overall life expectancy at birth, but also providing the conditions for the smallest possible gap between HALE and overall life expectancy. This is likely to involve both public health interventions as well as population-level adjustments towards healthier lifestyles.

EDUCATION

Singapore's education system is acknowledged as one of Asia's success stories (OECD, 2011). Significant improvements in educational attainment have raised the share of the resident population with tertiary education: In 2016, 30% of the population in their 20s who were not in full-time education had a university degree or more, up from 5% as recently as in 1990. More than half of the working age population have some form of tertiary educational qualification; and whilst there is still a large group of primarily older persons with lower than secondary school education (29%), 10% of the population aged 65 years and older have some form of tertiary educational qualification (Fig. 4).

Fig. 4. Singapore Resident Population 20+ Years by Age and Highest Educational Attainment (2016)

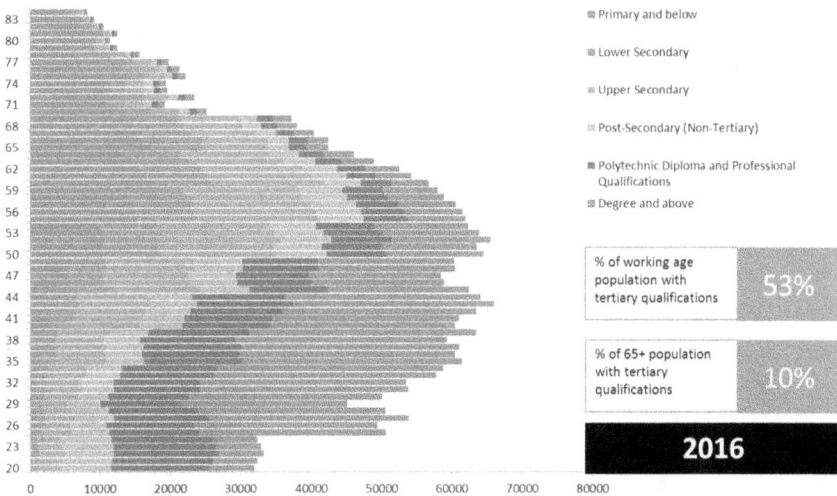

Source: Institute of Policy Studies estimates, based on data from Department of Statistics, Census of the Population, 2010.

With continued human capital investments, extrapolating the educational expansion achieved between 2000 and 2010 through to 2060 suggests that, by then, 87% of the working age resident population will have tertiary educational qualifications, as will 85% of the population aged 65 years and above (Fig. 5, next page). This represents a substantial increase in Singapore's human capital potential that can contribute to productivity gains, and improve individual and societal well-being.

Note that the effects of this educational dividend could be limited by diminishing returns to education, especially when the large majority of the population have advanced educational credentials, or from obsolescence of this accumulated human capital: an 85 year-old degree-holder in 2060 might have obtained her highest educational qualifications in the 20th century. The effect of ageist attitudes in the workplace, as well as more broadly in society could also restrict older worker participation rates.

Fig. 5. Singapore Resident Population 20+ Years by Age and Highest Educational Attainment (2060)

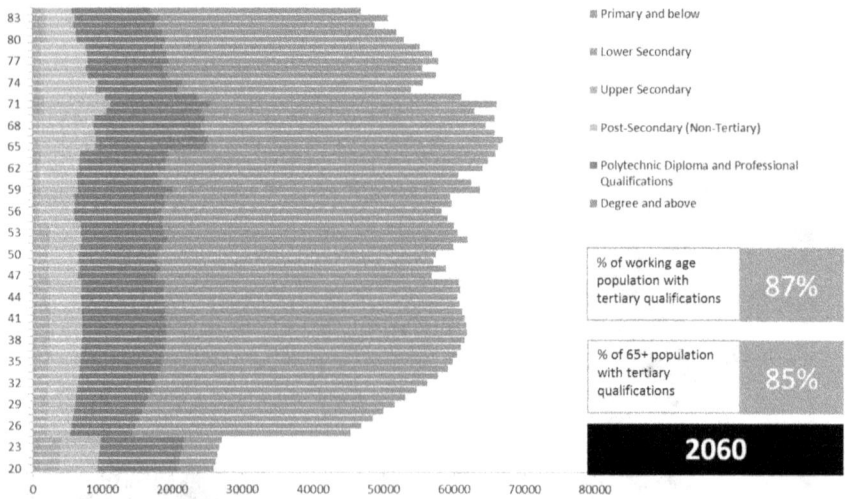

Source: Institute of Policy Studies projections, based on data from Department of Statistics, Census of the Population, 2000 and 2010.

SAVINGS AND INVESTMENTS

Over their life-course, those in the working ages typically produce more than they consume on average (accumulating a surplus), whilst children and the elderly consume more than they produce (resulting in a deficit). Societies have different approaches of re-allocating resources from surplus to deficit ages, but these methods generally follow two broad methods: through transfers or savings.

The first method relies on transfers from those in surplus ages to those in deficit ages. These transfers may be private, with familial transfers between parents to their children, and from adults to the elderly predominating especially in Asian societies such as in Singapore. Some of these private transfers may be between households, but intra-household transfers generally are more important. Other transfers may be intermediated by the public sector, with public programmes for education, health, housing and other social programmes financed out of taxation.

The second method depends on capital markets, where those in surplus ages accumulate capital, and in turn rely on their capital income (interest, dividends, rentals, and other investment income), or by liquidating their assets to support their consumption in old age when they are no longer working.

For Singaporean households, these savings will be in the form of Central Provident Fund contributions, the build-up of housing equity in the purchase of public or private property and other financial assets. This savings accumulation by the household sector can be seen in Fig. 6 (next page), with aggregate Singaporean household assets totalling $2.0 trillion as at September 2017, according to data from the Department of Statistics. Household assets have more than quadrupled since early 1995.

The Singapore government has also accumulated savings. The Net Investment Returns Contribution (NIRC) arising from public sector savings (derived from the accumulation of fiscal surpluses and net capital receipts of the government) contributed $14.4 billion, or 17% to the public sector budget in FY2016. In FY2014, the NIRC of $8.7 billion was a little in excess of the amount set aside in that fiscal year for the Pioneer Generation Fund ($8.3 billion).

Fig. 6. Household Assets (1Q1995–3Q2017)

In S$ millions

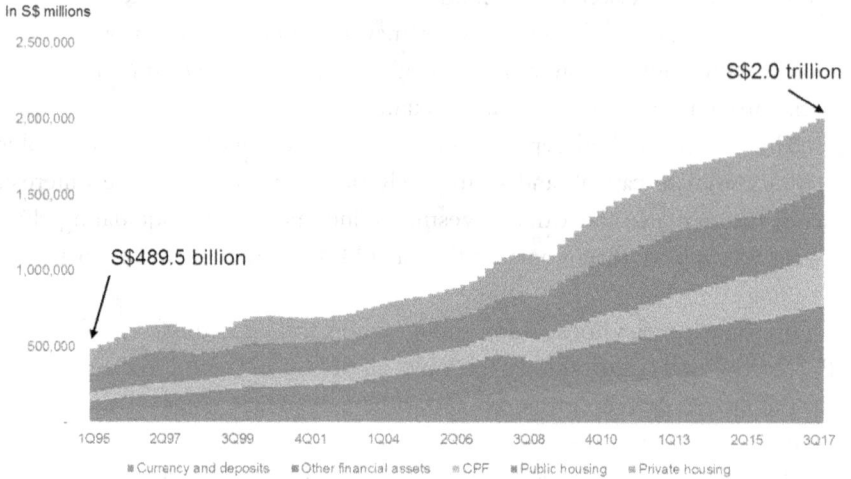

Source: Department of Statistics, 2017, Household Sector Balance Sheet (End of Period), Quarterly

TECHNOLOGICAL ADVANCEMENT COMPLEMENTS LONGEVITY DIVIDENDS

Greater investments from these accumulated savings into innovation and technology can boost these longevity dividends. Medical advancements focused in the area of underlying degenerative ageing processes could continue to add healthy and productive life-years to the population, whilst artificial intelligence (AI) and automation could complement an increasingly better-educated older workforce. Technological advancements in the area of robotics, AI and sensors could assist in the care of the elderly, and the negative effect of a shrinking and older workforce may be offset by the introduction of appropriate technology.

At the same time, innovation and technological advancement may yield unequal economic outcomes, with the immediate impact of the introduction of new, disruptive technologies likely to affect older workers most acutely.

HARNESSING LONGEVITY DIVIDENDS: POLICIES, INSTITUTIONS AND BEHAVIOURS

These demographic or longevity dividends are predicated on effective policies, institutions, norms and behaviours that allow the full economic and social benefit to be accrued. For example, if a country's capital markets are insufficiently well developed or managed, then savings may not be channelled effectively into productive investments, or the fruits of economic growth and innovation may become unevenly distributed leading to deep societal divisions.

Relying solely on individual savings to finance old-age consumption can also accentuate income and wealth inequalities, and may not be the most efficient means to hedge low probability, high-impact risks. Other mechanisms[4], such as tax-financed transfers and social risk pooling (or national insurance schemes) are alternative methods to finance old-age consumption that do not rely on familial assistance (that will become increasingly less reliable for more Singaporeans given demographic trends).

TAXATION-BASED FINANCING

Some countries rely heavily on taxes and public transfers to finance old-age consumption, with old-age social support in the form of tax-financed pensions representing 8.2% of OECD countries' GDP in 2016 (OECD, 2016). The equivalent in Singapore is 0.3% of GDP in FY2016, with the introduction of the Silver Support Scheme[5].

---

[4] All three methods of old-age consumption financing discussed here can be seen in Singapore's "3M+S" system of healthcare financing. Medisave is a mandatory savings scheme for medical expenditure administered as part of the Central Provident Fund system, whilst MediShield Life is a national health insurance scheme that provides lifelong coverage for hospitalisation. Medifund, the third "M", is a tax-financed endowment fund for patients facing financial difficulties with remaining medical expenditures after exhausting other means such as their savings and insurance. The "S" in "3M+S" refers to tax-funded subsidies provided by the government under means-tested eligibility criteria.

[5] The Silver Support Scheme is part of a wider suite of schemes (e.g., healthcare subsidies, GST Voucher) that the government has put in place in recent years to support the elderly Singaporeans aged 65 years and above who had low life-time

The social and political compact in Singapore is one based on low taxation levels in a progressive tax structure to keep the economy competitive, with targeted assistance via public transfers for those who need it the most. As expenditure on social needs rise, given the country's demographic trajectory, there is however a recognition that tax revenues will have to rise in tandem (Lee, 2012; Seow, 2017).

Tax increases will have an effect on economic competitiveness, an important matter for a global city-state such as Singapore with an open economy. The acceptance of tax increases [6] to finance increased social spending will depend on the type of taxes raised (e.g., consumption, income or estate); what the incremental fiscal revenues will be used for; how the increases are communicated; and, in some part, on the level of inter-generational solidarity amongst the population (given that tax-payers are mostly in the working-age groups).

SOCIAL RISK POOLING

Individuals have great difficulty hedging longevity risk. Whilst there is private insurance available to cover the risk of untimely death and catastrophic health shocks, there is much less that individuals can do to reduce the risk of outliving their retirement resources (in particular their financial and leasehold housing assets).

However, Singapore has well-established schemes that help Singaporeans with their longevity, such as the CPF LIFE or MediShield Life, which provide lifelong coverage for Singaporeans' retirement income needs and hospital-isation expenses respectively. These schemes are a form of social risk pooling, and provide an efficient and cost-effective way for people to manage the risks of catastrophic health shocks and longevity.

Other examples where social risk pooling can be applied are for employment shocks (e.g., unemployment or wage loss insurance schemes); for long-term care (e.g., universal long-term care insurance schemes); and

---

incomes and who have little or no family support. See more details here: https://www.silversupport.gov.sg/

[6] Or the increased utilisation of the returns from investing national reserves, which represented 20% of total government expenditure in FY2016.

other longevity risks such as housing (co-operative or community-based senior living programmes).

The concept of social risk pooling is predicated on some element of intra- and inter-generational solidarity in society. The issue of moral hazard in social risk pooling can be mitigated through effective policy design and social norms against bad behaviour by participants in the risk pool, whilst concerns over the actuarial fairness of premium pricing and reserving for future claims can be reduced if there is a strong sense of inter-generational solidarity in society.

WHAT ABOUT IMMIGRATION?

Immigration has historically been a major element in Singapore's population policies. As of June 2017, permanent resident and non-permanent resident foreigners comprised 39% of Singapore's total population of 5.6 million (Department of Statistics, 2017), up from 14% in 1990.

With Singapore's TFR at ultra-low[7] levels since 2003, the unwinding of the first demographic dividend amongst the local-born population is already in evidence (Fig. 7, next page). The Economic Support Ratio (ESR) amongst the Singaporean-born population peaked in the 2000s, with the increase in the ESR for the total resident population from 2000 to 2010 showing the positive effects of immigration on mitigating the economic impact of population ageing.

---

[7] Ultra-low fertility levels are defined as total fertility levels below 1.3 births per woman (Jones, 2012). In 2016, Singapore's resident total fertility rate (TFR) was 1.20, with 41,251 births recorded in the year. The peak year of births in Singapore was in 1958 with 62,495 births when the TFR was 6.20.

Fig. 7. Economic Support Ratio: by place of birth (1970–2010)

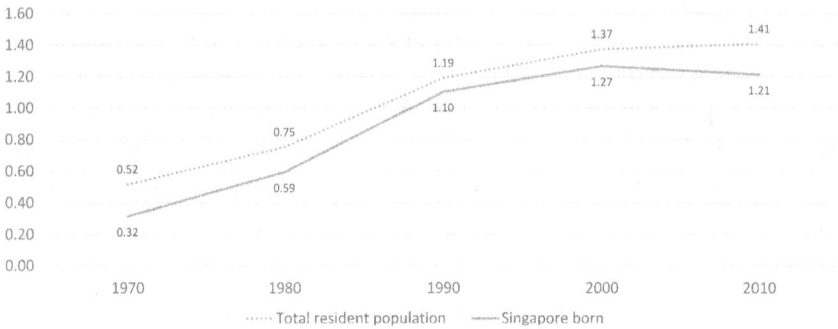

Source: Institute of Policy Studies estimates, using Population Census data published by Singapore Department of Statistics

There are limits, however, to how much immigration can offset the reversal of the first demographic dividend from population ageing. Immigrants also grow old, and an ever-larger intake of immigrants would be needed to prevent the total resident population ESR from declining in the future.

Whilst official government policy continues to be one of openness to immigration (especially of skilled labour) with an average annual intake of 30,000 new permanent residents, there is recognition that a well-calibrated immigration policy is only one measure to mitigate the economic effects of population ageing. As Prime Minister Lee said in his 2012 New Year's message: "A vibrant economy needs enough workers and talent, yet we run into physical and social constraints if we admit too many foreign workers too quickly. Diversity enriches our society, but only provided new arrivals adopt our values and culture."

ATTITUDES TOWARDS INTER-GENERATIONAL SOLIDARITY IN SOCIETY

Individual and societal choices about transfers (familial support, taxation or social risk pooling) and the effectiveness of savings-driven investment will be affected by the level of inter-generational solidarity in society. As such, in November and December 2017, the Institute of Policy Studies conducted a nationally representative telephone survey of 2,000 Singaporean citizens and permanent residents aged 21 years and above on their attitudes towards inter-generational issues and the use of national reserves, amongst other matters.

An initial review of the survey results indicates a few key areas of interest that will have particular relevance for the subject matters for discussion at Singapore Perspectives 2018:

- Notions of generational self-reliance and Singaporeans' bequest motivations.
- How should we pay for higher social spending on the elderly?
- After family, who should take care of the elderly in society?
- Ageism in the workplace

NOTIONS OF GENERATIONAL SELF-RELIANCE AND SINGAPOREANS' BEQUEST MOTIVATIONS

Survey respondents were asked whether they agreed or disagreed with (or had a neutral stance to) a series of statements about generational self-reliance and whether older generations should set aside their assets as an inheritance for the young.

The greatest proportion of respondents (41%) believe that each generation should take care of itself (Fig. 8, next page). However, **a surprising proportion (38%) disagreed with the statement, perhaps due to feelings of inter-generational solidarity**. Younger respondents aged below 40 years were more likely to disagree with the statement, whilst respondents aged 60 years and above were more likely to agree. This age differential is suggestive of an underlying notional sense of inter-generational solidarity amongst younger respondents, who would be expected to take care of older generations.

Fig. 8. Statement: "Each generation should take care of itself, without the need to be supported by other generations"[8]

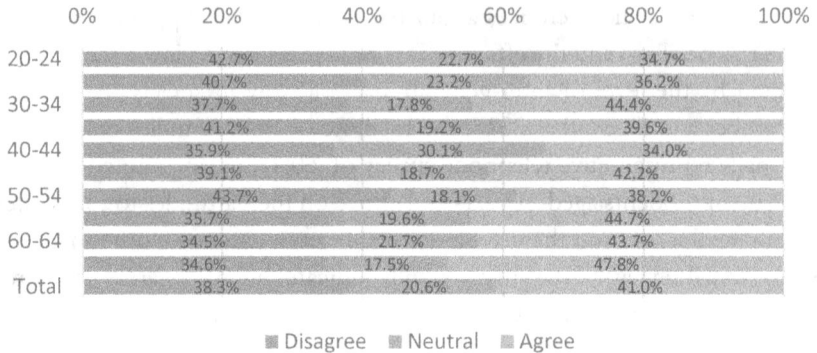

20-24	42.7%	22.7%	34.7%
	40.7%	23.2%	36.2%
30-34	37.7%	17.8%	44.4%
	41.2%	19.2%	39.6%
40-44	35.9%	30.1%	34.0%
	39.1%	18.7%	42.2%
50-54	43.7%	18.1%	38.2%
	35.7%	19.6%	44.7%
60-64	34.5%	21.7%	43.7%
	34.6%	17.5%	47.8%
Total	38.3%	20.6%	41.0%

■ Disagree ■ Neutral ■ Agree

Source: IPS Survey for Singapore Perspectives 2018

A number of academic studies have highlighted strong bequest motivations amongst Singaporeans (Phang, 2004; Asher & Kimura, 2015), especially for leaving property assets as an inheritance for the younger generation. However, **a surprising proportion of respondents in our survey (41%), disagreed with a statement that older generations should set aside assets as an inheritance for the young** (Fig. 9, next page). In particular, respondents aged 50-64 years were much more likely to disagree with this statement.

We therefore need to ask if the bequest motivation is less salient than commonly assumed, or is longevity risk forcing especially those Singaporeans in the "sandwiched" generation[9] to consider reserving their assets for their own old-age security?

---

[8] Respondents were asked to rate their responses to a series of statements on a five-point scale (1-Strongly Disagree, 2-Disagree, 3-Neutral, 4-Agree, 5-Strongly Agree). For the purposes of this initial analysis, we have aggregated the responses denoting agreement or disagreement. All the survey results here are presented weighted by age and housing type.

[9] Those in the "sandwiched" generation have a dual dependency: they may be caring for both the younger and the older generations.

Fig. 9. Statement: "Older generations should set aside money, property or other assets as inheritance for the young"

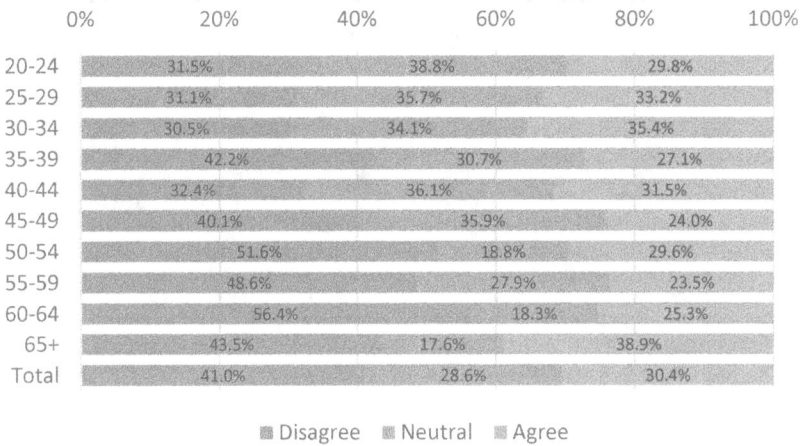

	Disagree	Neutral	Agree
20-24	31.5%	38.8%	29.8%
25-29	31.1%	35.7%	33.2%
30-34	30.5%	34.1%	35.4%
35-39	42.2%	30.7%	27.1%
40-44	32.4%	36.1%	31.5%
45-49	40.1%	35.9%	24.0%
50-54	51.6%	18.8%	29.6%
55-59	48.6%	27.9%	23.5%
60-64	56.4%	18.3%	25.3%
65+	43.5%	17.6%	38.9%
Total	41.0%	28.6%	30.4%

■ Disagree ■ Neutral ■ Agree

Source: IPS Survey for Singapore Perspectives 2018

HOW SHOULD WE PAY FOR HIGHER SOCIAL SPENDING ON THE ELDERLY?

Our survey posed some questions about increasing taxation (Fig. 10, next page) or using a larger share of the returns from investing national reserves (Fig. 11, next page) to finance higher social spending on the elderly. **We obtained mixed responses to both questions, with slightly more respondents (40%) disagreeing to paying higher taxes to fund increased social spending on the elderly.**

Whilst there were more neutral responses to the question on using a larger share of the returns from investing national reserves to finance higher social spending, more respondents agreed (37%) to the statement than disagreed with it (26%).

For both questions, respondents aged 45–64 years were more likely to disagree to paying higher taxes (Fig. 10) rather than tapping on national reserves, and to agree to using a larger share of the net investment returns to finance current social spending for the elderly. This age group experiences the highest tax burden and may be feeling the greatest uncertainty about financing their own post-retirement living expenses.

Fig. 10. Statement: "Would you be comfortable paying for higher social spending on the elderly through higher taxation instead of tapping on the national reserves?"

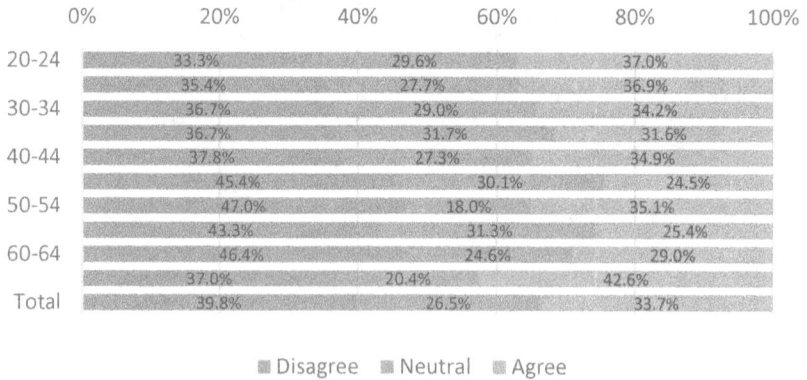

	Disagree	Neutral	Agree
20-24	33.3%	29.6%	37.0%
	35.4%	27.7%	36.9%
30-34	36.7%	29.0%	34.2%
	36.7%	31.7%	31.6%
40-44	37.8%	27.3%	34.9%
	45.4%	30.1%	24.5%
50-54	47.0%	18.0%	35.1%
	43.3%	31.3%	25.4%
60-64	46.4%	24.6%	29.0%
	37.0%	20.4%	42.6%
Total	39.8%	26.5%	33.7%

■ Disagree ■ Neutral ■ Agree

Source: IPS Survey for Singapore Perspectives 2018

Fig. 11. Statement: "Should Net Investment Returns (NIR) used to fund social expenditure for the current generation be increased, and the amount reserved for future generations be likewise decreased?"

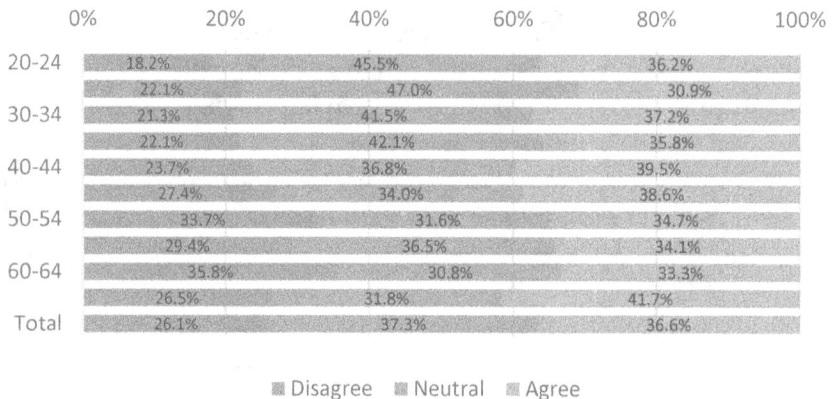

	Disagree	Neutral	Agree
20-24	18.2%	45.5%	36.2%
	22.1%	47.0%	30.9%
30-34	21.3%	41.5%	37.2%
	22.1%	42.1%	35.8%
40-44	23.7%	36.8%	39.5%
	27.4%	34.0%	38.6%
50-54	33.7%	31.6%	34.7%
	29.4%	36.5%	34.1%
60-64	35.8%	30.8%	33.3%
	26.5%	31.8%	41.7%
Total	26.1%	37.3%	36.6%

■ Disagree ■ Neutral ■ Agree

Source: IPS Survey for Singapore Perspectives 2018

AFTER FAMILY, WHO SHOULD TAKE CARE OF THE ELDERLY IN SOCIETY?

Three core principles underlie Singapore's approach to social welfare: (1) self-reliance, (2) family as the first line of social support, and (3) the concept of Many Helping Hands (MHH). Our survey asked respondents to rank four sectors (family, community, employers and the government) in order of importance of bearing the responsibility for taking care of older people.

Given strong familial ties, family was ranked first by 73% of respondents (Fig. 12). However, the government ranks second, with 69% of respondents ranking the government either first or second in importance of bearing the responsibility for taking care of older people. This is in contrast to the MHH concept, which incorporates the family as the first line of social support, followed by the community, whilst the role of the government is to establish the policy framework, and provide the underlying infrastructure and resources for the other sectors to deliver the care.

This survey result points to a disconnect in expectations about who might be responsible for providing care for the elderly in the absence of familial support, with people looking to the government to be the next in line to take care of the elderly, as opposed to the community under the MHH concept. It could also point to a belief that the capacity of the community to deliver support for the elderly is insufficient for this sector to bear this responsibility.

Fig. 12. Statement: "The responsibility for taking care of older people in society should be mainly borne by (Rank all options in order of importance)"

	Rank 1	Rank 2	Rank 3	Rank 4
Family	73.4	14.7	6.8	5.1
Community	3.0	24.9	45.4	26.8
Employers	2.0	13.3	27.6	57.1
Government	21.7	47.1	20.2	11.0

Source: IPS Survey for Singapore Perspectives 2018

AGEISM IN THE WORKPLACE: WHAT DO PEOPLE OF DIFFERENT AGES THINK?

Almost two-thirds of our survey respondents (66%) disagreed with the statement that older workers aged 55 and above do not face age discrimination. Whilst respondents aged 55–64 years were more likely to disagree with this statement (73% on average), almost two-thirds of younger respondents aged 25–54 years also disagreed with this statement. This shows that younger people are also aware of age discrimination in the employment market, and suggests some sympathy for older workers. Younger workers might also be voicing out fears of confronting age discrimination themselves when they are older (Fig. 13).

Fig. 13. Statement: "Older workers (aged 55 and above) in Singapore do not face age discrimination when looking for work"

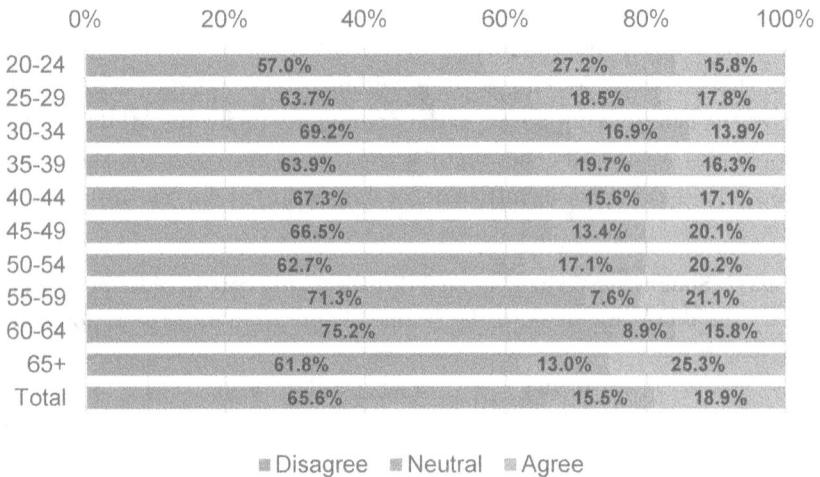

Age group	Disagree	Neutral	Agree
20-24	57.0%	27.2%	15.8%
25-29	63.7%	18.5%	17.8%
30-34	69.2%	16.9%	13.9%
35-39	63.9%	19.7%	16.3%
40-44	67.3%	15.6%	17.1%
45-49	66.5%	13.4%	20.1%
50-54	62.7%	17.1%	20.2%
55-59	71.3%	7.6%	21.1%
60-64	75.2%	8.9%	15.8%
65+	61.8%	13.0%	25.3%
Total	65.6%	15.5%	18.9%

■ Disagree ■ Neutral ■ Agree

Source: IPS Survey for Singapore Perspectives 2018

SINGAPORE PERSPECTIVES 2018 CONFERENCE, 22 JANUARY 2018: "TOGETHER"

We hope the Singapore Perspectives 2018 Conference, entitled "Together", will contribute to the national discourse on Singapore's demographic trajectory, and how, if demography is destiny, we may urgently shape the mind-sets, policies and decisions today for the best outcomes for our current and future generations.

This background paper provides some points for discussion during the conference, during which we hope to address these questions, amongst others:

What policies, institutions, and social and behavioural norms do we need to adapt, to enhance the standing of our longer-living Singaporeans as assets to society, rather than as a burden?

How do we sustain economic competitiveness and dynamism given an ageing workforce, and how to ensure maximum participation of Singapore's labour in economic growth?

How might the government apply taxation policies and utilise national reserves within the principles of fiscal sustainability and inter-generational equity, to promote a dynamic and inclusive economy and society?

How should our social care, social security and retirement funding systems be updated to enable Singaporeans to live longer lives successfully?

Will Global City Singapore be "no country for old men", or will it be a city-state for all ages?

To whom will Singapore belong, if the citizens of Singapore do not replace themselves?

REFERENCES

Asher, M. G., & Kimura, F. (2015). Strengthening Social Protection in East Asia. New York: Routledge.

Bloom, D. E., & Williamson, J. G. (1998). Demographic transitions and economic miracles in emerging Asia. The World Bank Economic Review, 12(3), 419–455.

Department of Statistics. (2017). Population Trends, 2017. Singapore: Department of Statistics.

Jones, G. W. (2012). Late marriage and low fertility in Singapore: The limits of policy. The Japanese Journal of Population, 10(1), 89–101.

Lee, H. L. (2012). Speech by Prime Minister Lee Hsien Loong at Economic Society of Singapore Annual Dinner 2012. Retrieved from: https://www.pmo.gov.sg/newsroom/speech-prime-minister-lee-hsien-loong-economic-society-singapore-annual-dinner

Mason, A. (2007). Demographic dividends: The past, the present and the future. Contributions to Economic Analysis, 281, 75–98.

Mason, A., & Lee, R. (2006). Reform and support systems for the elderly in developing countries: capturing the second demographic dividend. Genus, 62(2), 11–35.

OECD. (2011). Strong Performers and Successful Reformers in Education: Lessons from PISA for the United States. Paris: OECD Publishing. doi: http://dx.doi.org/10.1787/9789264096660-en.

OECD. (2016). Social Expenditure Update 2016: Social Spending Stays at Historically High Levels in Many Countries. Paris: OECD. Accessible at http://www.oecd.org/els/soc/OECD2016-Social-Expenditure-Update.pdf

Ogawa, N., Chawla, A., & Matsukura, R. (2009, April). Some new insights into the demographic transition and changing age structures in the ESCAP region. Asia-Pacific Population Journal, 24(1), 87–116.

Phang, S. Y. (2004). House prices and aggregate consumption: Do they move together? Evidence from Singapore. Journal of Housing Economics, 13(2), 101–119.

Seow, J. (2017, November 20). Singapore to raise taxes as govt spending increases. Retrieved from: https://www.straitstimes.com/singapore/spore-to-raise-taxes-as-govt-spending-increases

LINKS TO FURTHER READING

Pew Research Center. (2014, January). Attitudes about aging: A global perspective. Retrieved from: http://www.pewglobal.org/2014/01/30/attitudes-about-aging-a-global-perspective/

The Economist. (2017, July 6). Getting to grips with longevity: The Economist special report. Retrieved from: https://www.economist.com/news/special-report/21724745-ageing-populations-could-be-boon-rather-curse-happen-lot

Lee, R., & Mason, A. (Eds.). (2011). Population Aging and the Generational Economy: A Global Perspective. Cheltenham, U.K.: Edward Elgar. Retrieved from: https://idl-bnc-idrc.dspacedirect.org/bitstream/handle/10625/47092/IDL-47092.pdf?sequence=1

Harper, S. (2014). Economic and social implications of aging societies. Science, 346, 587–591. Retrieved from: http://www.eastscotbiodtp.ac.uk/eastbio_dev/sites/sbsweb2.bio.ed.ac.uk.eastbio_dev/files/Aging%20societies.pdf

Basso, H. (2015, April 9). How will an ageing population affect the economy? Retrieved from: https://www.weforum.org/agenda/2015/04/how-will-an-ageing-population-affect-the-economy/

Winkler, H. (2015, June 18). How will ageing populations affect politics? Retrieved from: https://www.weforum.org/agenda/2015/06/how-will-ageing-populations-affect-politics/

Bussolo, M., Koettl, J., & Sinnott, E. (2015). Golden Aging: Prospects for Healthy, Active and Prosperous Aging in Europe and Central Asia. Washington, D.C.: The World Bank. Retrieved from: https://openknowledge.worldbank.org/handle/10986/22018

The Economist. (2014, April 26). Age invaders. The Economist web edition. Retrieved from: https://www.economist.com/news/briefing/21601248-generation-old-people-about-change-global-economy-they-will-not-all-do-so

Some papers on Singapore which we hope will also help contribute to the discussion:

Kwok, A. (2006, October 1). Opinion: The Real Challenges of an Ageing Population. Ethos. Singapore, Civil Service College. Retrieved from: https://www.cscollege.gov.sg/Knowledge/Ethos/Issue%201%20Oct%20 2006/Pages/Opinion-The-Real-Challenges-of-an-Ageing-Population.aspx

Yap, M., & Gee, C. (2014). Population Outcomes: Singapore 2050. Singapore: Institute of Policy Studies. Retrieved from: https://lkyspp.nus. edu.sg/docs/default-source/ips/pos2050_web_final_3009141.pdf?sfvrsn= 1cb99e0b_2

Mathews, M., & Leong, T. (2014). Towards ageing well: Aspirations, challenges and initiatives. Working Papers, Institute of Policy Studies. Retrieved from: https://lkyspp.nus.edu.sg/docs/default-source/ips/c3A_ Web_Final_130115.pdf